The Green Family

Book of Household

Solutions

D1512558

The Green Family Book of Household Solutions

EARTH-FRIENDLY, MONEY-SAVING TIPS
AND FORMULAS FOR HEALTH AND HOME

Doug Donaldson

METRO BOOKS
New York

METRO BOOKS
New York

An Imprint of Sterling Publishing
387 Park Avenue South
New York, NY 10016

METRO BOOKS and the distinctive Metro Books logo are trademarks
of Sterling Publishing Co., Inc.

A POWERHOUSE PACKAGING & SUPPLY BOOK

This 2013 edition published by Metro Books by arrangement
with powerHouse Packaging & Supply, Inc.

Design by J. Longo and Lynne Yeamans

ISBN: 978-1-4351-4550-4

For information about custom editions, special sales, and premium
and corporate purchases, please contact Sterling Special Sales at
800-805-5489 or specialsales@sterlingpublishing.com.

1 3 5 7 9 10 8 6 4 2

www.sterlingpublishing.com

CONTENTS

INTRODUCTION:
Planting the Seeds of Change 6

CHAPTER 1:
Raising an Earth-Friendly Family 14

CHAPTER 2:
The Green Kitchen 34

CHAPTER 3:
Green Cleaning 53

CHAPTER 4:
The Green House 72

CHAPTER 5:
Lawn & Garden 102

CHAPTER 6:
Eco-Friendly Pets 136

CHAPTER 7:
Working & Traveling Green 162

CHAPTER 8:
Marketplace 184

Resources 198

About the Author 208

Planting the Seeds of Change

EVERY GENERATION WANTS THE BEST FUTURE FOR ITS KIDS. In today's world, knowing as we do that human activities have a demonstrable impact on the environment, that means living in an Earth-friendly way and raising a family that thinks and acts green. After all, when kindergarteners learn about the shrinking habitat of polar bears, it's hard to overlook the environmental consequences of our everyday choices.

Working together as a family to achieve a greener lifestyle is one of the best ways you can help bring about Earth-friendly changes. *The Green Family Book of Household Solutions* offers lots of simple ways to make your household, garden, and world a better place—while getting your kids involved in the process.

To help your family become more environmentally conscious, there are four important principles to adopt:

RECYCLE, REUSE, REDUCE, AND SAVE MONEY.

In the following pages you'll learn how to practice the 3 Rs—but first, let's talk about why.

RECYCLING HISTORY: WHAT'S OLD IS NEW AGAIN

Recycling isn't new. Since humans began making stuff, we've also been clever enough to continually repurpose that stuff. For instance, the ancient Romans recycled glass, melting down scrap glass to make new vessels. Around 1030 CE, waste paper in Japan was being repulped, made into new paper, and resold. And later, in Colonial America, some of Ben Franklin's publications were printed on recycled paper.

Throughout history, most recycling and repurposing was done on a household-by-household, small-scale basis. Tinkers scrounged metals to patch pots; women saved fabric scraps to make quilts. Recycling on a larger scale was rare.

During the Industrial Age, factories quickly and efficiently churned out so much stuff that there no longer seemed to be much of a need to recycle. However, with time, the terrible consequences of this attitude became increasingly apparent as our water and air became polluted, natural habitats became despoiled, species disappeared, and a host of toxins crept into our everyday environment.

"There are no passengers on spaceship earth. We are all crew."

—Marshall McLuhan, author and philosopher

Eventually, in response to the growing awareness that our planet was in danger, the environmental movement began to educate people and take action to stop pollution and preserve our natural resources. Such efforts led to the first Earth Day, on April 22, 1970. Governments and organizations around the world began addressing sustainability through the creation of agencies such as the the Environmental Protection Agency.

However, despite our growing environmental awareness, from 1960 to 2010, the amount of waste each person made increased from 2.7 to 4.4 pounds (1.2 kg to 2 kg) per day. In a typical year, we create about 250 million tons of trash.

Can one family make a difference when the scale is so large? Yes. Each year, more than 85 million tons of waste are recycled and composted, or about 1.51 pounds (0.68 kg) per person.

GREEN FACT... More than 1/3 of trash is recycled.

During the past three decades, the rate of individual recycling in North America and Europe has continually increased. In the United States in 1990, about 16 percent of waste was recycled. By 2000, the rate had increased to more than 28 percent, and by 2013 to more than 34 percent. In Europe, some countries recycle more than 60 percent of their waste products.

RECYCLE: OLD STUFF BECOMES NEW

RECYLE means to transform an item that would otherwise be waste into something reusable. In modern societies, it usually means to send an item to be cleaned, purified, and reprocessed (typically, paper, glass, aluminum, steel, or plastic) in a recycling facility.

Recycling is a key element of a greener lifestyle because it reduces consumption of energy (it generally takes less energy to recycle a product than to manufacture a new one), it causes less pollution than making something new, and it conserves raw materials. Finally, it reduces the amount of waste that has to be sent to landfills or incinerators.

Most communities now provide some form of recycling through curbside pickup or drop-off sites, local governmental services, or community organizations. The benefits from the simple act of complying with your local recycling regulations can help keep the air clean, reduce landfill accumulation, and save money and natural resources. When you recycle a product, it is broken

GREEN FACT... Every piece of paper adds up.

A year's worth of recycling waste paper in a building of 7,000 workers would be equal to removing the greenhouse emissions of 400 cars.

down into raw materials that can be reconstituted into new products. For example, in a process similar to making cotton candy, plastic bottles are spun into a fiber that's used to make carpet, fleece, and filling for clothing.

This book suggests lots of ways to make organizing and managing your recycling easier, and you'll also find plenty of inspiration and ideas for doing your own recycling of other items around the house and making it a family affair. For example, instead of simply donating your kids' old clothes, organize a neighborhood clothing swap (See page 21 for more details about having a successful clothing swap).

Recycling projects in the book are indicated with this icon

"I think the environment should be put in the category of our national security. Defense of our resources is just as important as defense abroad. Otherwise what is there to defend?"
–Robert Redford, actor, founder of the Sundance Film Festival, and environmental activist

REUSE: FIND ANOTHER
FUNCTION FOR OLD STUFF

REUSE means we keep on using an item over and over again until it cannot be used any more. For example, you might decide to wash your plastic cutlery instead of throwing it away after one picnic so that it can be used again. Some communities have created reuse centers, where items as diverse as building materials, books, plants, or school supplies are available to be picked up.

Reusing also means to repurpose or "upcycle" an item, such as using food scraps to make compost or turning an old bathtub into a planter or a shoebox into a container for art supplies.

Like recycling, reusing items saves energy and resources that would otherwise be used to make a new item, and reduces waste when your repurposed item does not find its way to a landfill. You'll find lots of reuse suggestions in these pages.

**Reuse ideas in the book
are indicated with this logo**

REDUCE: CUTTING DOWN THE AMOUNT OF STUFF YOU USE

REDUCE means you are finding ways to use fewer resources, to consume less, and to use the resources you do utilize more efficiently. Reducing is a key element of living a greener life. Conservation is the byword here: Energy and water are two major resources that you can use less of and use more efficiently; this book offers a wealth of tips that will help you reduce in both of those areas and more. From using fewer disposable plastic bags and more reusable containers to lowering your electric bills by turning off the juice, the conservation strategies you'll find herein will make you a greener family (and often reduce your household bills)!

Not creating waste is the best way to reduce it. Fortunately, manufacturers are looking to decrease the amount of waste and natural resources used to create products. On a household level, reducing is also a function of making green choices: to buy appliances that are rated for energy efficiency, to choose eco-friendly products over conventional ones, to purchase more in bulk to avoid excessive packaging, and to seek out reusable items. It also means making conscious choices about your usage and developing good habits, such as turning off the lights when you leave a room.

**Reduce ideas in the book
are indicated with this logo**

SAVE MONEY: GOOD FOR THE ENVIRONMENT MEANS GOOD FOR YOUR WALLET

You already know what saving money means! What you may not know is that thinking green has tremendous economic impact, both personally and on a larger scale. Recycling, reusing, and reducing help to create jobs. Recycling can generate six times the number of jobs and three times the amount of revenue as landfill disposal operations. And companies that buy recycled products and then resell them as new rely on such environmental efforts for all their business. Towns and cities that have to pay for landfill usage can save taxpayers millions of dollars by recycling.

Living a green life can save your family money, too. Reducing, reusing, and recycling are all money-saving strategies. Teaching your children to understand that items have value beyond their immediate use helps to slow the cycle of consumption. And in your daily lives you can save in obvious ways—some cities charge disposal fees based on the amount of trash thrown away. So, recycling can save on your garbage bill. Stores now often provide a discount for bringing your own reusable grocery bags. Throughout the following pages, you'll find many, many more ideas for saving money by recycling, reusing, and reducing.

Money-saving ideas in the book are indicated with this logo

CHAPTER ONE

Raising an Earth-Friendly Family

Raising a green family can be a real challenge in this age of convenience, but you can do it! Start by teaching children to respect nature, modeling a green lifestyle through your everyday choices, and helping kids understand that our actions do have an impact on the environment. Involving the kids in your family decision making and talking about why and how you are going to be a green family is the key to getting them motivated. Making it fun will keep them on the green path. This chapter has plenty of practical tips for developing eco-friendly family habits.

> **"Thanks to my mother, not a single cardboard box has found its way back into society. We receive gifts in boxes from stores that went out of business twenty years ago."**
>
> **–Erma Bombeck, humorist**

MODEL GREEN LIVING

 The most effective way to raise Earth-friendly children is to model green living yourself, so that the principles of reduce, reuse, and recycle are part of your family's daily life, and kids understand the importance of making green choices. Make conservation an active part of your life—turn off the power, use less water, lower the thermostat, buy less—and explain why you are doing these things.

- Teach children to respect and love nature—this can be as simple as regularly appreciating a sunset or sunflower with them or, more actively, keeping a photographic sunset diary or planting a garden together.

- Involve children in making green choices—at the grocery store, they can read labels and help find the least processed or packaged food; ask them to pick out a new fresh fruit or vegetable that is organically rather than conventionally grown.

- Leave the car at home—walk, bike, or take public transportation whenever possible (you and your kids will be healthier for the exercise, and the planet will be healthier, too).

- Set green family goals, and then work together to reach them. Repurpose or reuse an item that would have been thrown out, begin composting, or plan an eco-conscious vacation.

BUY MINDFULLY

 Since most of us cannot live off the grid, build our own homes from sustainable materials, and grow all our own food, we have to model green living in more manageable ways. One of those ways is to think carefully about what we buy and try to choose products that are truly eco-friendly. What does this mean? At minimum, products that are kind to the environment and safe for people and the planet.

Here is what to look for:

Nontoxic materials

Organic ingredients

Sustainably grown or raised ingredients

Recycled materials

Biodegradable ingredients

Get in the habit of reading labels and looking for these quali-fications before you buy. Ask the kids to help—when there is a choice between products, they can help evaluate which is greener.

> "Unless someone like you cares a whole awful lot, nothing is going to get better. It's not."
>
> **–Dr. Seuss, *The Lorax***

BRIGHT IDEA: REMEMBER TO TURN OFF LIGHTS

One of the simplest ways everyone in the family can save energy and money is to turn off the lights when they are leaving a room (that is not occupied by others, of course). For most of us, though, it's easier said than done. So, here are three strategies that'll help everyone remember to flip the switch:

UNPLUG LAMPS. Especially in rooms that aren't regularly used, such as the laundry room and guest room, only plug in lights when in use.

CREATE A REWARD SYSTEM. Have a savings jar into which you put a little bit of money every time a family member remembers to turn off the lights as they leave a rooom. Use the money to treat the family to a movie or ice cream.

INSTALL TIMERS. For families in which it just isn't practical to ask everyone to remember to turn off lights, the best approach may be to install timers that turn off lights at a specific time or motion detectors that turn on lights only when someone enters the room.

PACK A GREENER LUNCH WITH REUSABLE CONTAINERS

By some estimates, the average North American school kid's lunch generates 67 pounds (30 kg) of packaging waste per year. That is more than 18,000 pounds (almost 8,200 kg) yearly for an average-sized elementary school. So what's a lunch-packing kid to use instead? Start with a reusable lunchbox or bag. Replace plastic sandwich and snack bags with reusable cloth bags. Typically made from highly durable (and washable) oilcloth, fastened with Velcro, these sandwich bags are good-looking, clean, and, green—you can stock up on a half dozen and be set for the entire year. If you're minimally crafty and have access to a sewing machine, you can even make your own for a fraction of the cost. Invest in reusable drinking bottles and a thermos for soups and stews. Real cutlery and small cloth napkins complete the green lunch kit; just remind junior to bring it all home so you can pack another green lunch tomorrow.

> "A true conservationist is a man who knows that the world is not given by his fathers, but borrowed from his children."
>
> **—John James Audubon, ornithologist**

THE CRAFTS CORNER

   Arts and crafts offer tons of great opportunities for the green family! There are so many common household items that can be repurposed as arts and crafts materials—once you get in the habit of saving things in your crafts bin, you may find you never need to shop for these materials again. Some ideas for items that you can easily reuse in creative projects:

- **EGG CARTONS**
- **OLD GREETING** OR **HOLIDAY CARDS**
- **OLD MAGAZINES**
- **CARDBOARD (BOXES, TUBES)**
- **FABRIC SCRAPS**
- **RIBBON** AND **YARN ENDS**
- **MILK CARTONS**
- **PLASTIC CONTAINERS**
- **BOTTLE CAPS**
- **CANS**
- **BUTTONS**

STORAGE TIP: Turn old shoeboxes or plastic containers into craft-supply storage bins.

KEEP TRACK OF TRASH FOR ONE DAY

  It'll likely surprise you—and your kids—just how much garbage you throw away in one day. So, instead of tossing all your garbage in the trash can, use a clear plastic trash bag and have all the family members place all their trash in that bag for one day.

Once the day of trash collecting is finished, have a quick family meeting to talk about the household waste. Use a bathroom scale to weigh the trash. Talk about ways to reduce the amount of trash. Can your family recycle more or start composting? Then, in a month or two, do another trash-measuring day to see if your efforts have paid off.

Want to help raise awareness? Suggest to your kids' teachers that they try the trash-measuring exercise. Students will be amazed to see how much a whole class or school pitches in a day, and they can figure out creative ways to make their school greener.

"Remember that children, marriages, and flower gardens reflect the kind of care they get."

—H. Jackson Brown Jr., author of
Life's Little Instruction Book

ORGANIZE A CLOTHING SWAP

 Kids outgrow their clothes so quickly—but there's a greener way to update their closets than a shopping spree at the discount store. Why not organize a clothing swap with other like-minded parents? Your kids' old clothes can find a new home, and their wardrobes will get refreshed at the same time.

For best results, keep the group small (six to eight families is ideal) and invite guests to bring gently used (no stains or tears) garments they'd like to trade. Before people come over, assign big boxes or tables or even just areas of the room to categories, then put up signs (such as jeans, dresses, coats, etc.), so people can easily sort the clothes they bring into the same general types or sizes. When your guests arrive, allow some time for them to socialize and sort before the swapping begins. You can offer them stickers or Post-It notes so that they can mark which clothes they would like to take home—or just make it first come, first served. In case you have a situation where several people are keen on the same garment, consider having some ground rules so everyone knows beforehand how things will be settled fairly (drawing straws or a quick round of rock, paper, scissors are good choices).

When all is said and done, donate the leftovers to a local charity. And consider throwing an adult-clothing swap party, too!

LET WORMS EAT YOUR GARBAGE

  Kids and composting go together like dirt and water—especially if you can add worms to the mix. Composting with worms is a great activity for kids, and a perfect way to get them excited about composting (See page 110). You don't need a big yard or a compost pile to do worm composting; it's easy to do indoors with a simple worm composting kit, or you can make one yourself with items purchased at a hardware or garden store, or online. What you will need:

---

8 sheets of old newspaper

A 10-gallon (40 L) plastic or wooden bin with a lid

Drill with 1/4-inch (0.635 mm) bit

Shredded newspaper and cardboard

Food scraps, aka worm food (good choices are fruits and vegetables, coffee grounds and filters, tea bags, egg shells, bread, pasta, or rice, and citrus peels, but no dairy, oil, or meat)

1 lb (2.5 kg) *Eisenia fetida*, or red wiggler worms (available online)

---

1. Drill holes about every 3 inches (7.5 cm) in the lid of the bin

2. Fill the box about half full with "bedding" for the worms made of shredded paper and cardboard. Dampen (but don't soak) the bedding.

3. Add the red wrigglers.

4. Feed the worms by adding a layer of food scraps about 6 inches (15 cm) deep. Then, put a thin layer of bedding atop the food.

5. Wait a couple weeks and watch while your worms turn the food into "castings" or compost—when you have a good layer, scoop it out and use it to fertilize your garden.

"Our most basic common link is that we all inhabit this planet. We all breathe the same air. We all cherish our children's future. And we are all mortal."
—John F. Kennedy, 35th president of the United States

TURN SOAP SCRAPS INTO CRAYONS

  There are dozens of ways to use up those last few slivers of soap that always seem to collect in the bathroom, but making your own kid-friendly soap crayons is a win-win proposition because it's a surefire way to get your little one to linger in the bathtub. Here is a list of things you will need:

---

2 cups (240 g) bar soap, finely chopped

2-4 tablespoons (30–60 mL) warm water

1/2 teaspoon (2.5 mL) liquid food coloring
    or 1 tablespoon (15 mL) washable tempera paint

1 ice cube tray or other molds

GREEN FACT... Turning off the tap while brushing your teeth saves a surprising amount of water.

Most bathroom faucets pour about 2 gallons (7.5 L) of water per minute. When you turn off the tap while brushing your teeth or shaving, you can save about 200 gallons (750 L) of water per month.

1. Place soap and water in a bowl and use your hands to combine; work the mixture between your fingers until it becomes a smooth paste (if you're pressed for time, a food processor can do the job in seconds).

2. Before adding color, decide if you want pastel or deeper shades. For the former, drop in liquid food coloring till you achieve the desired shade; for brighter colors, add washable tempera paint.

3. Scoop out the paste and press the mixture into an ice cube tray or mold (or form into balls with your hands). Place the tray or mold in the freezer until crayons have fully hardened.

4. When you are ready to use the soap crayons, let them thaw out for a few moments till they are ready to use. Do test the crayons on a small area of your tub before letting your little Picasso go wild. Some tubs may absorb stains more easily.

"A society is defined not only by what it creates, but by what it refuses to destroy."
—John Sawhill, former executive at The Nature Conservancy

Green Family 101:
DISCOVER NATURE
IN YOUR BACKYARD

For kids, learning about shrinking glaciers and diminishing rainforests may be a bit abstract. Those things are thousands of miles away and may be hard to picture. Fortunately, your backyard (or neighborhood park) has its own ecosystem your child can study. Studying fireflies and bees provides a great deal of information about the health of the habitat, while growing simple plants gives kids the satisfaction of adding to the naturescape.

Tracking fireflies, observing bees, and growing flowers help your child to experience the sights, sounds, smells, and textures of nature directly. And what's even better: when your kids venture out, they will not only enrich themselves but can also contribute to real scientific knowledge.

FIREFLIES

On a warm evening when the fireflies start lighting up the twilight, head outside with the kids. Scientists don't know why, but it seems that firefly populations are declining. To find out more, volunteers are compiling data for scientists through the organization Firefly Watch. The information gathered from volunteers across the nation will help scientists analyze firefly populations. To help attract fireflies to your yard, turn off outside lights at dusk, add a water feature like a small pond or fountain, and avoid using pesticides in your garden. For more information and to sign up your junior scientist, check out the Boston Museum of Science site at mos.org/fireflywatch.

BEES

By counting the number and type of bees that visit flowers, your child can add to a valuable database of knowledge. In 2008, the Great Sunflower Project began to help track bees after their numbers began mysteriously diminishing. Volunteers observe flowers for 15 minutes, recording the types and numbers of bee visitors. And in addition to observing bee activity in your own backyard, the organization helps local groups get together to plant more sunflowers and provide additional observation. Go to greatsunflower.org for more info.

FLOWERS

One of the best ways to attract bees and other beneficial pollinators to your backyard is to grow the plants that attract them. Stands of sunflowers (or cosmos, tickseed, or purple coneflower) will do the trick. Choose a sunny spot in your garden (or at the local community garden)—most flowers prefer 6 to 8 hours of direct sun a day—to start your seeds. Water them and then watch them grow!

HAVE A FLAVORED-WATER TASTE-OFF

 Kids may think that H2O is boooooring and be tempted by high-sugar sodas or so-called "energy drinks" that contain not only sugar but also potent doses of caffeine. Help them steer clear of these calorie-laden, nutrient-deficient, unhealthy beverages by making water more exciting. By experimenting with adding natural flavors to water, you can help your kids find a healthier go-to drink. And as an environmental plus: You won't be buying lots of plastic bottles.

So, the next time you're at the grocery, stock up on a few fruits that you may not normally buy. When you get home, slice up the fruit, stir a few slices and/or squeeze some juice into glasses of water and have a family flavored-water experiment night.

Some of the fruits and flavors you may want to try:

Apples	Coconuts	Limes
Blackberries	Cucumbers	Oranges
Blueberries	Grapefruit	Pears
Cantaloupes	Grapes	Pineapples
Celery	Jicama	Tangerines
Cherries	Lemons	Watermelons

Keep a pitcher of your favorite flavored water in the refrigerator to encourage kids to grab a healthy drink whenever they're thirsty.

DRINK TAP WATER

 Drinking water is, well, essential for life. Staying hydrated keeps us healthy. In most places in North America, tap water is clean and safe to drink, and often delicious. In fact, expensive bottled water is frequently just local tap water that has been filtered and packaged into a fancy, often plastic, bottle. You can save money and prevent plastic bottles from clogging up landfills by drinking tap water and filling your family's reusable water bottles with it. An easy-to-install filter will take care of any concerns you may have about the quality and taste of the water. There are several types of filters that are suitable for home use:

CARAFE FILTERS: These jugs come with replaceable filters, and can be kept in the fridge. An inexpensive and reliable method.

FAUCET-MOUNTED FILTERS: These models screw onto the faucet, and allow you to switch between filtered and unfiltered water.

UNDER-SINK FILTERS: Installed out-of-sight, these are the most expensive but, especially if you have a large family, also the most efficient option.

TAKE A TOUR OF TOYLAND, THEN SHARE OR DONATE OLD TOYS

   Often kids' toys are measured by the bin. One bin for building blocks, another for action figures or dolls, and on and on and on! The bins build up, even as the kids lose interest in the toys. At least once a year (maybe make it an annual wintertime tradition before the holiday season), put the toys on parade to find out which ones your kids really still play with and like. Collect the toys your kids have outgrown and share them with friends' kids or donate them to a charity. This annual toy review is also a chance to keep an eye out for eco-friendly toys and to pull some potentially harmful toys out of those bins. For example, if there's a #7 stamped somewhere on the toy, there's a good chance that it contains bisphenol A (BPA), which has been linked to attention disorders and a host of other ailments.

"Children have to be educated, but they have also to be left to educate themselves."

—Ernest Dimnet, French writer and author of
The Art of Thinking

When it is time to purchase new toys, follow these tips for buying nontoxic:

- **Whenever possible, avoid plastic toys.**

- **Look for labels that indicate toys are free of toxic elements, such as "100 percent PVC-free," "no phthalates," "no formaldehyde," and "lead-free."**

- **Opt for toys made of wood, organic materials, or stainless steel, and that have been safely colored with water-based dye or nontoxic paint.**

- **Choose craft materials and art supplies that are labeled non-toxic.**

- **Search out toys that have met safety standards—look for a label that indicates the item has been tested, such as that from the American Society for Testing and Materials (ASTM).**

- **Check for safety warnings on the packaging, and follow them.**

- **Check recall lists at the Consumer Product Safety Commission site at cpsc.gov or at Health Canada's hc-sc.gc.ca.**

- **Buy toys with as little packaging as possible.**

Green Family 101:
MAKE MINIATURE ECOSYSTEMS

Kids, especially younger ones, may not grasp what the "environment" is or understand an "ecosystem," but this easy hands-on project can help little ones take a close-up look at nature in action. When kids help create these mini ecosystems, they'll also learn about plants and the environment from an entirely different part of the world.

Kids can help with or do just about every part of this fun project. For any of the options below, you'll need:

A 1-GALLON (3.7 L) GLASS JAR OR AQUARIUM

SMALL BAG OF ACTIVATED CHARCOAL (AVAILABLE AT PET-SUPPLY STORES)

SMALL BAG OF POTTING SOIL

POTTED PLANTS OF YOUR CHOICE (SEE BELOW)

1. Thoroughly clean and dry the container.
2. Place about a 1/2 inch (a little more than 1 cm) of charcoal in the bottom.

3. Add about 4 inches (10 cm) of potting soil above the charcoal.

4. Select a type of ecosystem and plant about three or four different kinds of plants. Here are some ecosystem choices, matching plants, and handy tips:

ECOSYSTEM	PLANTS	TIPS
DESERT	Cacti, aloe vera, prickly pear	Replace half the potting soil with sand. Avoid overwatering and leave top open
DECIDUOUS FOREST	Violets, strawberries, and wintergreens	Place in bright light but not direct sunlight
GRASSLAND	Prairie wildflower mix with a variety of grasses	Keep plants moist during blooming stage
RAIN FOREST	African violets, aluminum plants, and creeping Charlies	Remove plants from windowsills after dark
TUNDRA	Lichens, mosses, and small alpine plants	Place in a sunny window

CHAPTER TWO

The Green Kitchen

The kitchen is a great place to go green–healthier eating is frequently at the top of the priority list for families, and a green kitchen is a healthy one. Food choices and methods of preparation offer lots of opportunities to act in ways that are healthier for the planet and your family, from buying fresh, local, and organic food whenever possible to cooking efficiently at home. In addition to helping the environment, you will likely find that you are enjoying many more delicious meals!

In addition to food and cooking, you can also green your kitchen in other ways. The items you use in your kitchen, including appliances, utensils, and housewares, also offer many sustainable options.

USE YOUR KITCHEN

  Cooking your own food is a great way to avoid waste, eat healthy, and make Earth-friendly choices. Eat breakfast at home, bring a homemade lunch, and commit to cooking and dining at home 5 nights a week. You'll likely save money as well as the planet.

KICK THE FAST FOOD HABIT

  Heavily processed and refined foods are among the worst offenders in terms of environmental and personal health. Most food that we eat—unless we have personally harvested it and eaten it immediately—is somewhat processed. Minimally processed food has been washed, aged, dried, frozen, canned, cooked, or pasteurized to make it safer and more appetizing to eat, without destroying nutrients. A lightly processed food will have few ingredients on its label beyond the main item. But when food is more aggressively processed—altered with added fats and sugars, salt, and chemicals such as flavorings and colors, it loses nutritional value. Overprocessed foods have little in the way of vitamins, minerals, and fiber, but they usually have lots of calories and are packaged attractively and conveniently—and public health experts consider these ultra-processed foods a major factor in the rise in obesity and health problems that have accompanied it.

What to avoid:

> **White grains**, such as bread, rice, flour, and pasta; choose the whole, "brown" versions instead.

> **Trans-fats and hydrogenated oils**—if you see these on a label, skip that item.

> **Fast food and hyper-packaged food**—these are the mainstays of the global food industry, the items you tend to find at convenience stores, and are best avoided.

Instead, choose whole, fresh foods and cook them yourself.

EAT WHOLE AND FRESH FOODS

 Once you've committed to avoiding the temptations of overprocessed foods, you will find there is a delicious world of whole, fresh food awaiting. Here is a quick cheat sheet:

- **Whole fruits and vegetables**
- **Unrefined whole grains, such as brown rice, whole wheat bread, and quinoa**
- **Legumes such as beans, peas, and lentils (ideally, dried)**
- **Olive, peanut, and canola oil**
- **Fresh fish**
- **Lean, organically raised meats**
- **Organic, low or no-fat dairy products**

GREEN FACT... Eating organic produce reduces your pesticide exposure by as much as 90 percent.

Studies from both the U.S. Centers for Disease Control and Harvard University cite organic produce for decreasing exposure to pesticides that can cause a host of ailments, including some types of cancer and neurological damage.

EAT LOCAL

Just how far away does your food come from? The closer to you, the better.

Here's something to try: the 100-mile (160 km) diet. Do a little research and find out where the food comes from. Involve your family by posting a map and add pins that indicate farms that produce your fruits, vegetables, and meats.

You may be surprised at the variety and selection of local foods, as well. And your local research may lead to some family adventures to farms and markets you may not have known about.

GROW A KITCHEN GARDEN

Want to eat ultra-local? What's closer than your own backyard

  or windowsill? Starting a home vegetable or herb garden is an easy and wonderful way to eat green. Choose a sunny spot for your kitchen garden (at least 6 hours of direct sunlight is needed to successfully grow most vegetables). If you're gardening in containers, choose an organic potting mix. If you are digging your own dirt, you'll want to get the soil tested and then amend it with compost and organic fertilizer. Easy vegetables include lettuces, pole beans, zucchini, Swiss chard, and cherry tomatoes. Herbs such as basil, chives, mint, sage, thyme, and rosemary are simple to grow and good to have on hand. Look for organically grown seedlings at your farmers' market.

SUPPORT SUSTAINABLE AGRICULTURE

  "Sustainable" means farming practices that keep the environment (and the community) healthy. Sustainable farms do not use pesticides that are harmful to people or the land, and they avoid contaminating the water with chemicals. Instead they use natural methods like crop rotation to deal with weeds, diseases, and pests, and they keep the soil healthy and fertile with compost and erosion-preventing techniques.

Conventional agriculture, on the other hand, relies on pesticides and employs harmful chemicals and fertilizers to grow single crops, often for many years in the same soil, which eventually depletes its fertility. Conventional farming contaminates food and water with pesticides and nitrates.

You can support sustainable farming when you shop by buying local, organically grown produce.

"You don't have to cook fancy or complicated master-pieces—just good food from fresh ingredients."

-Julia Child, chef, TV personality, and author

MARK YOUR CALENDAR: MEATLESS MONDAYS

 Did you know that raising animals for meat uses more land, energy, and water than growing fruits and vegetables? And the United Nations' Food and Agriculture Organization estimates that the meat industry is responsible for almost 20 percent of greenhouse gas emissions worldwide! (Not to mention the issues associated with slaughtering and butchering, and the costs of transporting meat to the grocer.) With this information, even if your family is made up of committed carnivores, you may be able to convince them to set aside one day per week to go meatless.

Just how much does going meatless help the environment? In the United States, it takes about 40 calories of fossil-fuel energy to produce a single calorie of feed-lot beef. However, it only takes 2.2 calories of fossil fuel energy to bring one calorie of plant-based food to market. And eating one plant-based meal instead of a meat-based meal can save on carbon dioxide emissions and water.

Not only will it benefit the environment, it's also good for your family's health. Meat contains a lot of saturated fat, which can contribute to obesity, heart disease, and other health problems. Make Meatless Monday a family project by allowing kids to choose what vegetables to include. And if once a week is too tough for your family, start with once a month.

Green Family 101:
EAT IN-SEASON PRODUCE

Buying fruits and vegetables when they're in season is a great way to keep things green. Because food in season requires less travel time to get from farm to table, it's usually fresher and requires less energy to transport and store. Here's an at-a-glance guide to seasonal produce that will give you a general sense of what to expect in most temperate regions.

Of course, growing seasons are different depending on where you live and the varieties of plants that are available, so it is a great idea to find out what is in season in your region by talking to the growers at your local farmers' market about what you can expect to see from week to week. You can also find many charts online by searching for "seasonal produce."

IN-SEASON PRODUCE CHART

	Jan	Feb	Mar	Apr	May	Jun	Jul	Aug	Sep	Oct	Nov	Dec
Apples								■	■	■	■	■
Apricots					■	■	■					
Artichokes			■	■	■				■	■		
Asparagus				■	■	■						
Blackberries							■	■	■			
Broccoli	■	■	■							■	■	■
Brussels Sprouts	■	■	■						■	■	■	■

IN-SEASON PRODUCE CHART

	Jan	Feb	Mar	Apr	May	Jun	Jul	Aug	Sep	Oct	Nov	Dec
Butternut Squash										X	X	
Cauliflower	X	X	X	X	X	X			X	X	X	X
Cherries						X	X					
Cranberries									X	X	X	
Figs						X	X	X	X	X		
Garlic				X	X	X	X	X	X	X	X	X
Grapes								X	X	X	X	
Kale	X	X	X	X					X	X	X	X
Leeks	X	X	X	X	X		X	X	X	X	X	X
Melons						X	X	X	X			
Peaches						X	X	X	X			
Pears	X	X						X	X	X	X	X
Peas				X	X	X						
Peppers						X	X	X	X	X		
Romaine lettuce			X	X	X	X	X	X	X	X		
Spring Onions			X	X	X	X	X					
Strawberries				X	X	X						
Sunchokes	X	X	X							X	X	X
Sweet Potatoes									X	X	X	
Tomatoes							X	X	X	X		
Watermelon				X	X	X	X	X				
Zucchini						X	X	X	X			

KNOW YOUR DIET DEFINITIONS

 There are varying degrees of going meatless. Here's a list, ranking types of diet from most meat included to least:

FLEXITARIAN: A largely plant-based diet that occasionally includes meat.

MACROBIOTIC: A diet composed of whole grains, in-season fruit and vegetables, and occasional white meat and fish.

POLLOTARIAN: A diet that includes chicken but no other kinds of meat.

PESCETARIAN: A vegetarian diet that adds fish but no flesh from other animals.

LACTO-OVO VEGETARIAN: A plant-based diet that includes some dairy products and eggs.

VEGETARIAN: A diet that doesn't include any meat but may include dairy.

VEGAN: A diet that contains no animal-based foods at all.

"You must be the change you wish to see in this world."
—Mahatma Ghandi

KEEP YOUR FRIDGE FULL AND TIGHTLY CLOSED

  You may be surprised to discover that a full fridge operates more efficiently—this is because it has to work harder to cool empty space. You can fill empty spaces with glass or metal bottles or pitchers of water, which means you'll always have chilled water ready.

Another energy disaster is a loosely closed fridge—be sure everyone closes it tightly and that your seals are working properly. Test your closure by trapping a piece of paper in the door—if it falls out, it's time to replace those seals. For maximum energy efficiency, your refrigerator should be set to 37° F (3° C) and your freezer to 3° F (-16° C). And don't forget to sweep away the dust that accumulates behind and underneath the refrigerator—clean coils allow the machine to eliminate heat more efficiently and cycle less often.

Many homes have more than one refrigerator, though one is often an older model kept for extra food or drink storage. Today's ENERGY STAR refrigerators are so energy-efficient that replacing two old refrigerators with one new, larger fridge would reduce your power bill without sacrificing storage space.

MAKE A REUSABLE PICNIC SET

  In fine weather, it's tempting to pull together a picnic with disposable cups, plates, and cutlery. It's greener (and more stylish) to use one of those old-fashioned picnic sets, which are available at many home goods retailers. Better yet, make your own! Assemble it from old (ideally nonbreakable) cups, dinged cutlery, mismatched plates, or yard-sale pieces. If you must buy disposable, look for new, greener products that are intended to be easily recycled and are made with plant-based material that more readily decomposes.

GREEN FACT... With organic meat, you'll be 30 percent less likely to encounter antibiotic-resistant illness-causing germs.

Overuse of antibiotics on conventional farms can lead to the rise of super-germs. Organically raised meat is less likely to harbor these antibiotic-resistant strains.

HEALTHIER EATING:
PUT THE KIDS IN CHARGE (SORT OF)

  Buying healthy, organic foods is beside the point if your kids don't eat them. Get them excited about eating healthy by involving them in making the choices for your family meals. Here are four tips for getting kids on board:

PROVIDE TWO GOOD CHOICES When it's snack time, allow your kids to choose what they munch on, as long as the choices are two healthy options. For example, one choice could be some grapes and the other could be popcorn.

WAIT UNTIL THEY'RE HUNGRY When your kids are hungry, food will taste better. A platter of sliced veggies will be welcomed if you time the offering for right after they've been out playing, for instance.

LET THEM GO CRAZY IN THE PRODUCE AISLE Allow your kids to choose something totally at random from the produce aisle. They'll love the freedom and the whole family will get to discover a new fruit or vegetable.

PUT A CHEF'S HAT ON JUNIOR When kids are treated like their contributions are valuable, they're more engaged and will be more likely to eat the healthy food they're helping to prepare. Give your children specific jobs they can easily handle without burning or cutting themselves, such as washing veggies and mixing.

Green Family 101:
COOKING TO PRESERVE NUTRIENTS

Taking the time to carefully select your food and making wise choices at the grocery is more meaningful if you cook in a way that maintains the nutrients. Certain cooking methods are better for preserving good-for-you vitamins and minerals in food, while other cooking techniques can actually add fat and calories. Here's your guide to cooking to maximize your food's nutritional value:

BOILING Though easy, boiling is not an ideal way to cook vegetables. It drains almost all of the antioxidants from most vegetables and often leaves them mushy and flavorless. The exception is carrots, which receive a slight boost in nutritional value from boiling. Zucchini, peas, and cauliflower are especially prone to losing nutrients through boiling. If you must boil your vegetables, keep the water and add it to a broth. That way, you'll still reap some nutrients from the boiled veggies.

SAUTÉEING Cooking veggies over a high heat for a short amount of time helps maintain the antioxidant content.

> **"Our food should be our medicine and our medicine should be our food."**
>
> **-Hippocrates, ancient Greek physician**

FRYING Nutrient values of vegetables can drop up to 50 percent when fried. Plus, frying heaps on unhealthy calories and fat. For example, frying a 3-ounce (85 g) serving of potatoes adds more than 100 calories and doubles the fat content, compared to baking.

MICROWAVING The microwave is an excellent choice for preserving nutrients in most fresh food. Multiple studies show that microwaved vegetables retain more nutrients than those steamed or boiled.

PAN GRILLING One of the best ways to cook veggies is to use a griddle. Grilling preserves a high amount of antioxidants and helps provide a succulent flavor. Do use a cast-iron pan or griddle that doesn't have a chemical-based nonstick coating.

BAKING Baking is a mixed bag as far as bumping up or decreasing antioxidant value. For example, corn, spinach, eggplant, and green beans receive boosts in antioxidant levels from baking. But other veggies, such as peas, celery, beets, and Brussels sprouts, all had decreases in antioxidants.

STEAMING For vegetables such as broccoli and zucchini, steaming is an excellent way to keep the nutrients intact. One tip for ensuring you get the most nutritional value from steamed vegetables: serve them tossed with olive oil. This helps your body absorb the antioxidants better.

SAVE ENERGY WHILE COOKING

  Try these tips to cut down your energy consumption while cooking.

- Use the right-size pot for your electric stove burner. Cooking on a larger element with a smaller pot could waste 40 percent or more heat.

- Secure pots with tightly fitting lids.

- Make your oven do double duty by cooking two dishes at once whenever possible.

- Reheat with a microwave, which can save as much as 80 percent energy compared to the oven.

- When boiling water, use a lid to help keep the heat in. Bonus: the water will boil quicker.

- Consider buying a pressure cooker, which can reduce cooking time and save energy.

POWER DOWN

  If you plug all your small appliances into a single power strip, you'll be able to flip the switch to turn them all off at once, avoiding "vampire" power use.

WASH DISHES THE GREEN WAY

  You'll save energy if you wait until the dishwasher is full to run it—and operating it at night is usually cheaper than running it during the day. If you have a delay on your machine, set it to run several hours after you've gone to bed. You can also turn off the heated drying option to save even more.

For a small load, wash dishes the old-fashioned way: by hand! If you have a divided sink, fill one side with soapy water and the other with clear rinsing water. If you have a single sink, use a small tub or bowl to hold your soapy water. Don't leave the water running while you wash!

GREEN FACT... Low-fat yogurt may not be as healthy as it sounds.

While it may seem like a good idea for you and your kids to snack on yogurt, you have to read labels carefully. Some low-fat yogurt contains as many grams of sugar as a snack cake. A better yogurt option is plain Greek yogurt, and if you need it sweeter, plop in a dollop of honey or homemade jam.

BYOB—BRING YOUR OWN BAG

 With the plethora of free, reusable tote bags being given out for promotional purposes these days, there is really no excuse for using plastic. Your best bet is to always keep your own bags handy—stuff a few into your car, purse, or backpack, and you'll be prepared wherever you are. There are plenty of options that fold up into small packets that are easy and convenient to carry. When shopping (for anything), just remember to use the bags you brought. Another plus: Lots of stores are now giving cash back to those who use their own bags. For those plastic bags that you inevitably do end up with, make them do double-, triple-, or more duty. At least they won't have lived a single-serving life. Then, drop them off at a plastic-bag recycling bin, which can often be found at the entrance to a grocer.

> **"I did not become a vegetarian for my health, I did it for the health of the chickens."**
> **-Isaac Bashevis Singer, author of *A Day of Pleasure: Stories of a Boy Growing Up in Warsaw***

FORGET ONE AND DONE: GIVE UP PAPER TOWELS

   Paper towels impact the environment in so many ways, including destroying trees, processing and bleaching the fibers with harmful chemicals, and packaging and shipping them to stores—all for a single-use product. Do the planet a big favor by switching to washable, reusable rags. Slice up old towels, sheets, and even clothing to make your own. Yard sales may yield old dishtowels and cloth napkins, which make excellent, washable replacements for paper towels.

Organize your collection of sustainable cloths by designating particular rags for certain uses and storing them where needed. For example, keep kitchen-cleaning rags under the kitchen sink and only use them there. Old towels are perfect for heavy-duty jobs; keep them in a bucket in the garage, garden shed, or by the back door.

NO MORE PAPER NAPKINS

   Paper napkins, just like paper towels, are a convenience that is not worth the cost to the environment—and breaking your paper napkin habit can even save you money! If you have a collection of cloth napkins already (not the fancy party sort but everyday ones), then you're all set; if you don't, you can purchase them inexpensively or start nabbing them at yard sales and flea markets. Substitute these for paper napkins and you'll be doing the environment a favor.

An easy way to get your family on board: make or purchase a napkin ring for every family member—each one should be different, so that each person has his or her own napkin ring that is not easily confused with anyone else's. After each meal (unless it was something terribly messy), shake out and return the napkin to its ring, and use it again for the next meal. You'll have to decide how frequently to change them, based on your own family's meals and neatness levels.

If your family simply cannot commit to using cloth napkins, opt for napkins made from recycled paper. Choose products with 100% recycled content and a high amount of "post-consumer recycled content." That means not only is the napkin made from recycled content (manufactured scraps and waste, for example) but it is made from materials that have been recycled by consumers.

CHAPTER THREE

Green Cleaning

We'd like to think that when we clean, we're eliminating germs, creating a healthier environment, and keeping our families safe. But if you're using conventionally formulated, commercial cleaning supplies, it's very likely you're doing exactly the opposite.

Many commercial cleaning products are actually harmful both to the environment and to people because they contain toxic chemicals. Rather than subject your family and your home to these dangerous products, why not opt for equally effective, much healthier options that are made from nontoxic ingredients or even make them yourself? This chapter contains loads of cleaning recipes that you can easily concoct in your own kitchen and use around the house with confidence that you really are cleaning up!

> "Let the clean air blow the cobwebs from your body. Air is medicine."
>
> **–Lillian Russell, actress and women's suffrage advocate**

Green Family 101:

Lurking behind the cleaning closet door, under the sink, or in your basement may be some of the least eco-friendly substances in your house, masquerading as helpful products. Just look at the labels. You'll likely see words such as "flammable," "toxic," or "poison." Think about it: if you're spreading these chemicals on your floors, countertops, and tables, you may be unintentionally creating a harmful chemical cocktail in your own home.

Many of the chemicals used in conventional cleaning supplies have been linked to health concerns, including cancer, migraines, seizures, and rashes. The fumes from these cleaners actually pollute the air in your home and expose your family to danger. In addition, many of the ingredients that are not specifically toxic to humans are terrible for the environment, polluting water and air both when they are made and when they are used. Some ingredients to avoid include:

- Alkylphenol ethoxylates
- Glycol ethers
- Monoethanolamine
- Nonylphen
- Nonoxynol within ingredients
- Petroleum distillates
- Phenol and cresol
- Phosphates

Throw out all the conventional cleaners that contain any of these ingredients or any safety warnings and start fresh! Especially if you haven't gone through your cleaning supplies in a while, now's a good time for a cleaning closet audit. You can get rid of potentially toxic stuff that you don't use and figure out what supplies you need to replace with more environmentally friendly alternatives. Be sure children aren't around when you do this. In addition to the toxic products, look out for these:

AIR FRESHENERS Whether aerosol or solid, most commercial air-fresheners are prime examples of "cleaning" products that actually add something unclean to your environment. Fresh air is clean; these products pollute. Many contain a nasty mix of chemicals that can include benzene, d-limonene, and formaldehyde. Get rid of them and open your windows, or make your own air freshening product.

SCENTED PRODUCTS On labels, they promise "springtime air" or "mountain pastures," but the chemicals used to create those fragrances may contain phthalates, which are harmful.

CHLORINE BLEACH A standard in many cleaning closets, chlorine bleach is an extremely harsh chemical that can trigger strong skin reactions, eye problems, and even affect breathing. Also, bleach can interact with other chemicals, possibly creating even more harmful substances.

TOSS 'EM SAFELY

 DON'T throw conventional cleaning products in the trash or pour them down the drain, as you will be compounding the problem. **DO** contact your local waste removal authorities to ask how to get rid of these products. Most municipalities have collection plans and drop-off sites where you can safely dispose of your potentially toxic cleaning supplies.

STOCK UP ON GREEN CLEANING SUPPLIES

 Now that you've gotten rid of the nasty cleaning products, what should you use instead? Here is your handy green cleaning ingredient list:

- BAKING SODA

- LEMONS

- VINEGAR (WHITE, DISTILLED)

- DISH SOAP (PHOSPHATE-FREE)

- VEGETABLE-BASED SOAP

- OLIVE OIL

- SALT

- SPRAY BOTTLES

- GLASS JARS WITH LIDS

- RAGS

HOW TO SHOP FOR GREEN CLEANING PRODUCTS

Today, many companies know that consumers would prefer to buy nontoxic, Earth-friendly products. Some of these companies are careful to formulate products that are not harmful to the Earth or its residents, from manufacture through end-use. However, other companies cynically exploit customers' desires to be green, and sell products that are either toxic or at best, untested—these products often feature claims that sound good but are actually meaningless. This practice is known as "greenwashing." How can you choose the truly green products?

- Don't be fooled by unsubstantiated claims: words such as "natural," "eco-friendly," "green," or even "nontoxic" may be used without regulation, so they are not necessarily meaningful guides to the substances within. Instead, look for specific claims, including "phosphate-free," "no pthalates," or "readily biodegradable."

- Opt for products that have been certified by a reputable agency, such as the EPA.

- Look for products that are minimally packaged. A green company is likely to put some effort into packaging their products carefully, without excess materials, for example, or by using recycled or recyclable materials.

SKIP THE ANTIBACTERIAL CLEANERS

 The active ingredient in most antibacterial cleansers is Triclosan, which is considered a likely culprit in the creation of antibiotic-resistant strains of bacteria. Research has found that this chemical may also pose a risk of disrupting normal hormone function. Instead, use nontoxic disinfecting cleansers that you make yourself (see below) or purchase green products, and put some muscle into your cleaning efforts rather than relying on the product alone.

GREEN FACT... Many conventional cleaning products contain compounds that can damage lungs.

Made with chemicals such as formaldehyde and chloroform that can pollute your household air, these products are best avoided. A handy resource for finding safer options is the Environmental Working Group Cleaner Database at ewg.org/guides/cleaners. The site grades thousands of products. Stick with those that scored an A or B on the safety scale.

YOUR ALL-PURPOSE GREEN CLEANING SOLUTIONS

 Are you hanging on to your old, toxic products in the belief that some germs, stains, or dirty jobs are just too tough for green solutions? Think again. You can keep your home perfectly clean and germ-free without harsh and potentially dangerous chemicals. Below are 22 home cleaning solutions that you can make and use, confident in the knowledge that they are nontoxic, and safe to use–both for you and the environment.

Another bonus: These safe, homemade cleaners will cost you a fraction of store-bought cleaners. And they tend to smell better, too!

ALL-PURPOSE CLEANERS

CITRUS-VINEGAR SOLUTION

2 TO 3 CUPS (200 TO 300 G) LEFTOVER LEMON PEEL (OR OTHER CITRUS FRUIT PEELS)

2 CUPS (500ML) VINEGAR

Place the lemon peels in a large, open-mouthed jar, then cover with vinegar. Put the lid on the jar and allow the solution to sit for about 4 weeks in a cool, dark place, shaking about once a week. Strain through a cheesecloth and discard peels. Great for countertops and most surfaces, including glass.

BAKING SODA FORMULA

1 CUP (250 ML) WARM WATER

1/4 CUP (60 ML) DISHWASHING LIQUID

16 OUNCES (450 G) BAKING SODA

Good for just about any nonporous surface, this cleaner makes a good all-around scrub for stuck-on grime. Mix the warm water and dishwashing liquid together in a bowl, then add the baking soda, stirring until smooth. Pour into a jar and it's ready to use. Let it sit for 30 minutes before putting a lid on it. Shake between uses.

EASY DISINFECTANT

1/4 CUP (60 ML) VINEGAR

To disinfect countertops, use undiluted vinegar—no water need-ed. Pour the vinegar onto a clean cloth, wipe down the surface to be disinfected, and allow to air-dry. The vinegar's acidity kills most bacteria and is ideal for surfaces exposed to raw meat.

HEAVY DUTY DISINFECTANT

1 CUP 3% HYDROGEN PEROXIDE SOLUTION

For extra cleansing, foll ow the vinegar wipe with hydrogen per-oxide, after testing to be sure it won't react with the surface.

SIMPLY VINEGAR

1 PART WHITE VINEGAR

1 TO 9 PARTS WATER

Swish ingredients together in a spray bottle, squirt, and wipe. The amount of vinegar can be increased based on the toughness of the cleanup. Use this solution for light stains and general grime cleanup.

KITCHEN CLEANERS

STOVETOP CLEANER

2 CUPS (500 ML) HOT WATER

1 TABLESPOON (15 ML) PHOSPHATE-FREE DISH LIQUID

1 TEASPOON (5 ML) BORAX

Blend ingredients together in a spray bottle, then spray on mess, allowing it to soak in for at least 15 minutes. Wipe off with a cloth, repeat if necessary.

REFRIGERATOR SCRUB

1/4 CUP (75 G) SALT

1/4 CUP (55 G) BAKING SODA

Blend the salt and baking soda, and pour the mixture over spills in the fridge. Then with a sponge soaked in warm water, gently scrub. The mixture won't scratch the refrigerator surfaces.

CUTTING BOARD CLEANER

1/4 CUP (75 G) SALT

First, wipe off the board with a damp sponge, then spread the salt over the surface. Allow the salt to stay on the board for a few minutes. Rub with the sponge in small sections to remove stains, then rinse with hot water and allow to air-dry.

GREEN FACT... Vinegar is effective against bacteria.

A study published in the 1997 issue of the journal *Food Microbiology* showed that spraying vinegar and then spraying hydrogen peroxide on produce killed a majority of *E. coli*, *Salmonella*, *Shigella*, and *Listeria* bacteria.

MICROWAVE CLEANER

1/2 BOWL WATER

1/2 LEMON

Put the lemon in the bowl of water inside the microwave and turn it on high for about 2 minutes or until the water becomes steamy. Let the microwave door stay closed for 5 minute, then wipe down the inside of the microwave with a sponge.

CAST-IRON PAN CLEANER

1/2 CUP SALT (150 G) SALT

1/4 CUP (60 ML) VEGETABLE OIL

Start by washing off the surface of the pan with hot water. Scrape as clean as you can with a gentle implement such as a silicone spatula or wooden spoon. Next, heat the skillet for about 30 seconds over medium heat. Mix the salt and vegetable oil on the skillet, scouring with paper towels until clean. Rinse off with hot water and dry on medium heat.

OVEN CLEANER

BOX OF BAKING SODA

WATER IN SPRAY BOTTLE

Cover the bottom of the oven with baking soda, then spritz with water until somewhat damp. Allow to sit for about 8 hours, scrape, and wipe clean.

METAL COOKWARE SCRUB

1 TABLESPOON (8G) FLOUR

1 TABLESPOON (18G) SALT

1 TABLESPOON (15ML) VINEGAR

Blend the mixture into a paste. Apply the paste to a sponge and use it to scrub your metal cookware. Rinse with warm water and dry with a soft towel.

GREEN FACT... Lemons contain about 5 percent citric acid.

The acid content in lemons makes them all-natural, cleaning superstars. Lemons can be used to lift stains as varied as grass, mustard, coffee, and sweat. In addition, lemons have bleaching properties that help to brighten whatever's being cleaned.

GLASS COFFEEPOT CLEANER

1/2 CUP (150G) SALT

LEMON SLICES

ICE

WATER

Fill the coffeepot a little over halfway to the top with ice, some lemon slices, salt, and water. Swirl the mixture around for a few minutes. After pouring the mixture out, be sure to rinse a few times before using again.

"We generate our own environment. We get exactly what we deserve. How can we resent a life we've created ourselves? Who's to blame, who's to credit but us? Who can change it, anytime we wish, but us?"

—Richard Bach, writer and author of
Jonathan Livingston Seagull

BATHROOM BUSTERS

TUB SCRUB

1/4 CUP (55 G) BAKING SODA

1/2 LEMON

Sprinkle baking soda in the tub, putting more on troublesome spots. With the cut side of a lemon, scrub the tub, squeezing the lemon to release juice. Rinse when finished.

TILE CLEANER

1/2 CUP (110 G) BAKING SODA

4 TABLESPOONS (60 ML) PHOSPHATE-FREE DISH LIQUID

Put baking soda in a bowl, then pour in liquid soap, stirring until the mixture thickens. It should be about the consistency of cake frosting. Use a sponge to apply to bathroom tiles, then wipe tiles clean. Clean up any residue with a clean, damp cloth.

"When we heal the earth, we heal ourselves."
–David Orr, environmentalist and university professor

SHOWERHEAD LIME-DEPOSIT REMOVER

1 CUP (250 ML) VINEGAR

Remove the showerhead with a wrench (remember, "lefty-loosey") and place in a cup of vinegar for a night. You can also soak a rag with vinegar, and wrap it around the showerhead.

WOOD FLOOR CLEANER

1/2 CUP TO 1 CUP (125 TO 250 ML) VINEGAR

1 GALLON (4 L) WARM WATER

Sweep first and then for a deeper clean use this mixture with a damp mop. If you have previously used oil soap, use closer to a cup or 250ml of vinegar. A bonus to using vinegar: It'll help keep water spots from forming as it dries.

TOILET BOWL CLEANER

1 CUP (250 ML) VINEGAR

1/2 CUP (110 G) BAKING SODA

First, pour vinegar into the toilet bowl and let it sit for about an hour. Next, sprinkle a toilet-scrubbing brush with the baking soda and rub it around the inside of the toilet and under the rim. Add more baking soda for tougher stains.

EVERYWHERE ELSE CLEANING

WINDOW AND GLASS CLEANER

1/4 CUP (60 ML) VINEGAR

1/2 TEASPOON (3 ML) LIQUID SOAP

2 CUPS (500 ML) WATER

Blend ingredients in a spray bottle and shake well. Spray cleaner on glass and use a squeegee, cleaning it between wipes with a cotton cloth.

CARPET STAIN REMOVER

1 HANDFUL SALT

1/2 CUP (125 ML) COLD WATER

1/2 CUP (125 ML) HYDROGEN PEROXIDE

First, cover the stain with salt, then mix the cold water and hydrogen peroxide in a bowl. Dab a clean cloth in the liquid and dab the salt until it clumps. Blot stain with clean cloth (repeat).

DUST BUSTER AND FURNITURE POLISHER

2 TABLESPOONS (30 ML) LEMON JUICE

10 DROPS LEMON OIL

2-4 DROPS OLIVE OIL

Avoid chemical-laden cleaners with this easy formula. Mix ingredients in a bowl, dampen a clean cloth, and wipe dust away.

SANITIZER

1/2 CUP (125 ML) VODKA

PEEL OF 1 LEMON

For doorknobs or other high-touch areas in the house such as light switches, this is a great germ-buster. Pour the vodka into a spritzer bottle and drop in the peel of a lemon. Allow to sit in a cool, dark place for a few days. Shake and spray. You'll have a sanitizing, yet pleasant-smelling, formula for household cleaning.

"I can remember when the air was clean and sex was dirty."

–George Burns, comedian

HOW TO PLAY THE DRAIN GAME—AND WIN!

  When your drain is clogged, it's not a pretty situation. Water backs up, nothing will go down, and there may even be a bad smell, too. You want to fix it—quick. Plunging might help a little, but for those tough clogs, it's not enough. The result? Lots of people feel they have no choice but to turn to harsh chemicals.

If you take a look at the average drain cleaner label, however, you'll find thoroughly scary warnings about the ingredients being poisonous and able to burn skin and eyes. Definitely not something you want to use.

So, what's the green solution to a clogged drain? Think snake. Invest in a drain auger, or snake, a handy tool that clean drains without the use of harsh chemicals. Drain augers have claws or ridges that can grab the hair, food, or other gunk that is causing the clog and remove it from the drain. They are not expensive, and if you purchase a reasonably good-quality one, it'll last for years, which means you won't be buying those jugs full of toxic chemicals over and over.

For a ounce of prevention, avoid pouring grease and coffee grinds in the drains, and use a hair trap. A kettle of boiling water poured down the drain weekly might help too.

SWEEP AWAY DISPOSABLE FLOOR CLEANERS

 Those plastic-handled floor sweepers are sure easy to use, aren't they? Just press the cloths into the little claw-like indentations in each corner, sweep, then throw away. Convenient, right? At least, that's what the manufacturers would have you believe. The truth is, along with the waste, those cleaning cloths contain chemicals. To avoid throwing away box after box of cleaning pads, and save yourself some money, here are a few greener ideas for using the floor cleaner:

- Substitute old rags or towels. They'll slip into those claws just as easily and you can wash and reuse them.

- Knit or crochet a covering. With a little Velcro or some buttons, create a knit covering for the head of the sweeper. You can remove it, wash it, and continue using it.

MOPPING SOLUTION

HALF A GALLON (2 L) WARM WATER

1/2 CUP (125 ML) OF WHITE DISTILLED VINEGAR

If prefer the wet pads used in the floor cleaner, don't worry—you can make your own very easily. As a substitute for the wet versions of cleaning pads, stir up a mixture of warm water and distilled vinegar. Soak a rag, wrap it around the mop head, and go!

CHAPTER FOUR

The Green House

Think of your house as a miniature Earth, with its own ecosystems that interact with the larger ecosystem that is our planet. The main elements of your home environment are water, air, energy (heat and light), and waste—and, of course, the living beings who call it home.

To live in a more sustainable way in your home, you'll want to focus on managing your ecosystems in ways that reduce consumption and waste, and thereby lower your environmental impact. Every year, the average North American household consumes more than 100,000 gallons (379,000 L) of water and generates approximately 22 tons (20 t) of carbon dioxide.

You can lower your environmental impact by paying special attention to reducing your water and power usage; lessening the amount of waste you produce; preventing pollution of your environment; and creating greener surroundings for your family. Not only will your family indeed be healthier, but the good effects of your efforts will reach far beyond your home. The information in this chapter provides strategies and practical advice for how do it.

DO AN ENVIRONMENTAL IMPACT CALCULATION

A great way to get started on greening your home is to take a close look at how you live now, and figure out your current environmental footprint. The two overarching categories to look at are resource consumption, i.e., energy and water usage, and waste production, which includes carbon dioxide and greenhouse gas emissions, as well as your trash and wastewater production. One of the easiest ways to get started is to try one of the numerous online calculators that will help you to gauge your home's environmental footprint. Alternatively, you can call on professional help by hiring a local environmental impact consultant. In either case, you will end up with a better understanding of how your lifestyle affects the environment and what you can do to lower your impact.

GREEN FACT... Refrigerators use the most energy of just about any appliance.

The refrigerator consumes the most energy in the kitchen. Swapping out an old, less-efficient refrigerator can save enough energy to light a household for about four months. Look for a refrigerator with the Energy Star certification. These fridges are about 20 to 30 percent more efficient than other models meeting minimum energy efficiency standards.

Green Family 101:
WATER CONSERVATION

It's easy to take water for granted. After all, our planet is mostly water—how can it be scarce? In fact, less than 3 percent of the Earth's water is fresh water, and less than 1 percent of that is available for human use—the rest is frozen in icecaps and glaciers or deep beneath the surface of the planet, out of reach. As the world's population continues to grow, more water is needed. Yet water is a finite resource—the Earth is a closed system, and the amount of water stays the same. Nature has recycled it over and over again!

In many parts of the world, people have little access to clean, safe drinking water. In some areas, people must walk for hours to find a source of water. Even in areas where clean water is plentiful, usage of water has increased dramatically over the years, as populations grow and agriculture, commerce, and industry require ever-greater amounts. The cost of maintaining access to clean water is also on the rise, as producing and transporting clean water and processing wastewater require large amounts of energy.

Pollution is a problem around the world, as lakes, rivers, and other water sources are becoming contaminated. Habitat destruction means that wetlands, areas that naturally purify groundwater, are being lost. Climate change is causing drought in some areas and floods elsewhere. These threats to our water supply make it particularly important that we learn to conserve the water we have.

In most North American homes, clean water flows freely, and we use it with abandon. Helping your family members to be more aware of their water usage is the first step toward becoming water wise. Next, start a family water conservation plan that:

- **Lowers your overall water use**

- **Recycles water where possible**

- **Reduces water waste**

- **Prevents pollution**

Get the kids involved in making these decisions—if they understand how your family's actions can save the planet's water supply and know how they can make a difference, you will ensure they're on board!

"Organic buildings are the strength and lightness of the spider's spinning, buildings qualified by light, bred by native character to environment, married to the ground."

—Frank Lloyd Wright, architect

CONSERVE WATER ONE DRIP AT A TIME

  One very good place to start saving water is that annoying leaky faucet! A faucet that drips about 10 times per minute will leak about a gallon (3 L) per day. There are about 15,000 drips in a gallon of water! Wasted water from a leaky faucet adds up quickly. By fixing leaks, you'll save a significant amount of water, not only trimming your household bills, but lowering the amount of wastewater coming from your home, which in turn will help your local water processing plant to expend less energy to purify and pump water.

KEEP IT COOL IN THE FRIDGE

  A glass of cool water is so refreshing. It's all too easy to simply run the water till it reaches a nice, cool temperature. But allowing water to pour out of a faucet for 5 minutes sends a valuable amount of fresh water straight down the drain. (It also uses about as much energy as a 60-watt lightbulb that's left on for 14 hours.) Instead of letting the water run until it's cool enough to drink, pour your drinking water into a pitcher and store it in the refrigerator. You won't have to wait since you'll have a ready supply of chilled water for drinking, and you'll save money while conserving water.

KITCHEN WATER SMARTS

  There are lots of ways to use water more efficiently in your kitchen. Here are just a few tips that are easy to implement.

Use the lowest dishwasher settings. You're already running your dishwasher only when it's fully loaded, right? Be sure to choose settings for the lightest load/shortest wash cycle.

Replace aerators. Even if you don't want to replace your faucet system for a more efficient model, you can install an efficient aerator (which is in the cap of the spigot) simply by unscrewing the old one and cinching on the new. You don't need to know anything about plumbing, and it doesn't cost much.

Thaw frozen foods in the refrigerator. A stream of warm water may be a quick way to defrost frozen food, but it wastes lots of water. Instead, thaw foods a day beforehand in the refrigerator.

Reuse water when you can. Does your dog need some fresh water in his dish? Don't just dump the old H_2O down the drain. Pour it over plants or use it to rinse off dirty shoes.

"Home is an invention on which no one has yet improved."

–Ann Douglas, author

BRUSH YOUR TEETH THE DRY WAY

 Most kids know this one already: never let the water run while brushing your teeth! Since the average bathroom faucet flows at a rate of about 2 gallons (about 7.5 L) a minute, if you turn it off while brushing, you may save as much as 8 gallons (30 L) of water per day per person. Wet the brush, then partly fill a glass for rinsing. (You can apply this trick when shaving, too—no need to run water for rinsing a razor!)

DON'T FLUSH MONEY DOWN THE TOILET

 Go ahead and snicker. But toilets are not a laughing matter. About 30 percent of residential indoor water consumption is due to toilet usage. You can reduce the flow with a low-tech trick: fill a plastic water bottle (or two) with small stones or sand and water, so that it sinks, then place it in the tank. This will reduce the amount of water needed per flush. You can also purchase simple devices that do the same thing, such as fill cycle diverters or tank banks.

> "Our houses are such unwieldy property that we are often imprisoned rather than housed by them."
>
> **–Henry David Thoreau**

GET A NEW-FANGLED TOILET

Changing your inefficient toilet to one that uses less water can save up to $2,000 for a family of four over the lifetime of the toilet. In addition to the water flushed with routine use, toilets are often the culprits for leaks and other wastefulness. When it's time to replace your old toilet, consider these options:

DUAL-FLUSH Even if you don't want to replace your whole toilet, kits are available to convert your old toilet to a dual-flush. This option allows you to use less water for liquid-only and more water for solid wastes.

HIGH-EFFICIENCY These toilets use less water than government standards. For example, in the United States, toilets with the WaterSense label use 20 percent less water than those that simply meet federal standards. For an average family of four, a WaterSense toilet can save 4,000 gallons (15,000 L) of water a year.

COMPOSTING A form of toilet that's designed to use little to no water, a composting toilet uses the natural process of decomposition. These systems incorporate sawdust or peat moss to absorb odor and aid the decomposition process. Composting toilets are often a good choice for areas without water service.

GET WET WITHOUT GETTING SOAKED

 What's more relaxing than a nice, hot shower? But you may feel less relaxed when you learn that about 17 percent of a household's water consumption is from showering. In the United States alone, more than 1.2 trillion gallons (4.5 trillion L) of water go down the drain from showers.

For a more efficient shower, purchase a low-flow showerhead fixture that reduces the flow of water yet still gives the sensation of a full-force shower. Such high-efficiency shower fixtures are not expensive and can save up to 60 percent of the water you'd otherwise use.

When shopping for a high-efficiency showerhead, look for one that has a flow rate of less than 2.5 gallons (9.4 L) per minute (gpm).

GREEN FACT... Prerinsing dishes before putting them in the dishwasher wastes water.

Instead of prerising dishes before washing, give them a good scraping. Recent innovations in dishwashers and detergents eliminates the needs for prerising. And if the dishes have stuck-on goo that's sat overnight, use the dishwasher's rinse feature, which uses less water than hand rinsing.

6 GREENER WAYS TO WASH CLOTHES

  Cleaning your clothes with some environment-saving tips means you can also save some money. Here's how:

DIAL TEMP TO COLD. Save energy by switching the washing machine temperature to cold—your clothes will get just as clean. For conventional washing machines, about 90 percent of the energy used for washing clothes is for heating the water.

BUY A WATER-EFFICIENT MACHINE. An average washing machine may use more than 40 gallons (151 L) a load. High-efficiency machines require 35 to 50 percent less water and use half the energy. Choose an Energy Star-efficient model.

LOWER THE LEVEL. Often, your machine's controls will let you use lower water levels. Some newer washing machines will analyze the load automatically and use just enough water.

DON'T DO PARTIAL LOADS. Wait until you have a full load of laundry before using the washer and dryer.

BE MINIMAL BUT BULKY. When considering laundry items, look for those that have the least amount of packaging. Buying these items in bulk or concentrated forms also saves on packaging.

TURN DOWN DRYING TIME. When your dryer spins already-dry clothes, it wastes money and energy. Be sure the dryer's moisture sensor is on or choose the efficient setting, which is usually marked.

CUT THE CHEMICALS FROM YOUR LAUNDRY

Maybe your great-grandmother did laundry the old-fashioned way, using a washing board to scrub the clothes, then air-drying the lot. While today's methods are less labor-intensive, the cleaning products they involve may be loaded with chemicals that can be hazardous to your health and that of the planet.

While you probably are not ready to go back to great-grandma's washing methods, you can swap out some high-chemical laundry products for some safer alternatives. Here's how:

PRODUCT	A BETTER ALTERNATIVE
Chlorine bleach	Lemon juice; vinegar; oxygen-based brightener that doesn't contain chlorine
Dryer sheets	Line-dry clothes; use dryer balls with essential oils for scent
Fabric softener	During the rinse cycle, add a cup of white vinegar

LET IT RAIN, RAIN, RAIN—INTO YOUR BARREL

   Collecting rainwater with a barrel is one of the easiest ways to help the environment while saving money. With a rain barrel, you store water that would have flowed to storm drains, sparing the sewage system in your community. A 55-gallon (208 L) rain barrel can save about 1,300 gallons (4,921 L) of water over the course of a summer.

Water from a rain barrel is perfect for watering lawns and gardens, washing cars, and other exterior cleaning chores. Using this free source of water can significantly reduce the amount of water you'd normally have to pay for.

Rain barrels are simple to install and are easy to maintain. And in addition to providing a free source of water, they'll also reduce energy needs for pumping water to households. Think that doesn't add up? It requires about 1.5 kilowatts of electricity to move 1,000 gallons (3,785 L) of water to a household.

Depending on your level of handiness, you can either build a rain barrel from scratch or buy one—they are commonly available at garden centers, hardware stores, and online, and range from simple plastic or wooden barrels to decorative planter styles or models that connect to irrigation systems.

RUN HOT AND COOL, EFFICIENTLY

 Heating and cooling account for about half the energy used by most homes. As far as the money you spend for energy, heating and cooling top the bill, as well. So, when you want to save money, reduce your energy consumption, and be more environmentally friendly, the first places you should look at are your heating and cooling systems. Understanding what those systems do and making sure they are operating as efficiently as possible are the key aspects of making your home's eco-systems sustainable.

Whether you are a home handyperson who does all your own repairs or someone who calls in the pros at the first sign of trouble, there are maintenance tasks that are beyond the skills of most average homeowners. Your heating and cooling systems require regular professional maintenance, and it's important to keep to a schedule with a service provider who knows your home and will help you keep your systems running efficiently. In the spring and fall, make an appointment for a licensed contractor to inspect your heating and cooling system. Such regular maintenance will help lower your carbon footprint, prevent costly repairs, and keep you comfortable year-round.

HEATING AND COOLING ZONES

 There are several strategies you can use to minimize the energy required to heat and cool your home:

PROGRAM YOUR THERMOSTAT. Inexpensive and easy to install, a programmable thermostat allows you to vary the temperature according to a pre-set schedule. You can store and repeat multiple daily settings (for example, you can lower the temperature during the day when family members are out and raise it when they get home). When you need to, you can manually override the settings, then switch back.

CHOOSE ENERGY-EFFICIENT TEMPERATURES. During the cold months, set your thermostat to 68° F (20° C) while you're awake (wear a sweater if you feel chilly) and lower while you're asleep. When the temperatures rise, set the thermostat to 78° F (25° C) for the most energy-efficient cooling.

ZONE OUT. Only heat and cool the parts of your home that you are regularly using; less-used areas, such as guest rooms, can be closed off until you need them. Rooms such as mud rooms or unfinished basements don't need heating or cooling at all.

ENROLL IN A GREEN ENERGY PROGRAM. Offered in many municipalities, these programs allow customers to choose to have all or part of their electricity generated from renewable resources. Enrollment and billing go through your usual provider, but your home's energy will come from sustainable sources.

REGULARLY CHECK AIR FILTERS

 All heating and cooling systems have air filters designed to trap lint, dust, and other airborne particles that are constantly sucked in. When the filters become clogged, it makes the whole system work harder. A good rule of thumb: Check your filter at least every three months, and more often in high-use months, and clean or replace it as needed.

GREEN FACT... Retrofitting 1 out of 100 homes with water-efficient fixtures is equal to the annual greenhouse gas emissions of about 15,000 cars.

Faucets that pour out more than 2.5 gallons (9.5 L) per minute are considered inefficient. If 1 out of 100 homes replaced older faucets with efficient ones that have a flow rate of 1.5 gallons (5.5 L) per minute, that would save 80,000 tons (approximately 72,500 t) of greenhouse gas emissions, or about 100 million kilowatt hours of electricity per year.

THE BEAUTY OF EFFICIENT WINDOWS

 Everyone loves a large window that lets in light and frames a view. However, most windows are also a major source of drafts and heated/cooled air loss. Making your windows more energy efficient is a great way to green your home. Start by evaluating the windows you have and making them as efficient as possible. Caulk and plug any cracks or leaks in the frames, sash, and seals. Apply weatherstripping. Storm windows or double- and triple-paned windows will help in colder climates. If your windows are very old or you are still experiencing significant drafts, it may be time to replace them with new windows.

If you decide to install new windows, look for Energy Star–rated products. You will also want to pay attention to U-factor and Solar Heat Gain Co-efficient (SHGC).

- **U-FACTOR** is the rate at which glass conducts heat. In cooler climates, aim for a U-factor of 0.30 to 0.35 to help keep heat indoors during cold months. In hot climates, look for a U-factor of around 0.60 to keep you cool in hot weather.

- **SHCG** measures how much solar radiation is transferred through your window glass as heat. In cooler areas, it is recommended that you choose windows with an SHGC of 0.35 to 0.40. In warmer areas, look for windows with an SHGC of 0.27 to 0.30.

AVOID UNNECESSARY HEAT LOSS

  Help your heating system do its job more efficiently by searching out sources of heat loss that you may not have thought about.

- **USE HEAVY CURTAINS.** Draperies can prevent heat from leaving via the windows. In sunny rooms, open the curtains and let the sun heat up the place; when the sun is gone, close curtains to help keep warm air in.

- **CIRCULATE THE WARM AIR.** Hot air rises; use a ceiling fan to help move the warmth down to where the people are.

- **WARM THE FLOORS.** Use area rugs and carpeting to add a layer of warmth.

GREEN FACT... Washing dishes with a dishwasher usually saves more water than washing by hand.

The new Energy Star dishwashers are designed to make the most use of water, using about 4 gallons (15 L) per cycle. Using one of these dishwashers instead of hand washing can save about 5,000 gallons (about 19,000 L) of water each year—not to mention about 230 hours of time you'd otherwise spend in front of the sink.

KEEP THE COOL AIR INSIDE

  When it's warm outside, try these strategies to help your home stay cool.

- **SEAL LEAKS.** Avoid leakage of your cooled air by the same methods you prevented heat loss: insulation and sealing of leaky spots in your home.

- **CROSS VENTILATE.** Whenever the outdoor temps are not too high, let cooling breezes pass freely through rooms by creating cross-ventilation.

- **CREATE AIRFLOW PATHS.** Open windows and doors inside the home to create movement of air from one side of a room to the other, or from room to room.

- **INSTALL CEILING FANS.** In bedrooms and living areas, ceiling fans can keep air moving.

- **KEEP THE SUNSHINE OUT.** When the sun is high, close curtains and blinds; reflective toning on windows can also help. Shade windows from the outside with trees, awnings, and external blinds.

> "A house is a machine for living in."
> **—Le Corbusier, architect and writer**

HOT WATER SMARTS

For most homes, heating water is one of the top three energy expenses. Up to one-quarter of the amount of energy your home uses may be devoted to heating water. You can get hot water faster and reduce how much you pay for water heating by following these tips:

- **CHECK FOR LEAKS.** Your water heater can develop leaks in several locations, including the cold water intake or hot water output pipes, the relief valve, or the tank itself. Check the heater regularly for leakage and repair immediately.

- **WRAP IT UP.** Cover your water heater with an insulation blanket to keep the heat in. It's also worth it to insulate approximately the first 6 feet (2 m) of the pipes connected to the heater. Just be sure not to cover the thermostat or the top, bottom, or burner compartments of gas or oil water heaters.

- **DRAIN REGULARLY.** About every three months, drain about 1 quart (1 L) from the hot water tank. This trick will prolong the life of your water heater by helping to remove sediment that can impede the heating process.

- **LOWER THE THERMOSTAT.** Set the hot water heater thermostat to 120° F (48° C).

LET THE SUN HEAT YOUR WATER

 Using the power of the sun to heat your water makes lots of sense—you don't have to pay to use it and you won't have to rely on the electric company, which means you'll save money and reduce consumption.

If you have a south-facing roof that is not blocked by trees or buildings, you may want to install a solar water heater. There are several variations on the basic system. In each method, solar panels are heated by the sun. Some systems use a solar panel that transfers heat to a special fluid, which is then circulated through pipes to heat the coils in the water tank. Other systems use a water tank that is mounted above solar panels, which heat the water as it moves into the home. If you live in a warm climate, you may opt for a solar batch collector, in which water is pumped up to a solar storage tank on the roof, where it is heated by the sun. Then you just use the hot water as needed. (Make sure your roof is sufficiently strong to support the weight of the stored water and the tank.)

"The use of solar energy has not been opened up because the oil industry does not own the sun."

–Ralph Nader

BUTTON UP YOUR ATTIC TO REDUCE DRAFTS

  Your attic can be a heat and cooling thief. Especially if you live in an old home, chances are you don't have enough insulation in your attic. An uninsulated or under-insulated attic means that the air you are paying to cool or heat is leaking out. In the summer, cool air escapes from your main living areas into those rafters and beyond, while in the winter precious heat is lost. Fortunately, you can easily insulate your attic. Some tips for better attic insulation:

- **MEASURE DEPTH.** How can you tell if your attic needs better insulation? If there is less than 11 inches (28 cm) of fiberglass or rock wool or less than 8 inches (20 cm) of cellulose, you should probably add more insulation. When it is higher than the floor joists, you probably have enough.

- **PAY ATTENTION TO ACCESS POINTS.** Whether you access your attic through a regular door or a pull-down staircase, the area around the entrance to the attic often lacks adequate air sealing. Be sure to insulate around these entrances, and seal any cracks with caulk.

- **PUT UP A BARRIER.** In hot climates, a type of insulation called "radiant barrier" can act like a heat mirror. For example, when heat from a hot roof penetrates the attic, a sheet of radiant barrier insulation can reflect the heat outward, preventing it from transferring to the lower parts of your home.

SMALL SPACES, BIG LEAKS

 Insulation is an extremely important tool in energy saving, as it helps you keep warm air indoors in cold temperatures and keep hot air out when it's hot outside. It's easy to overlook the many small yet drafty places in your home that can make it much less energy efficient than you'd like. Some of the small, but common, places include:

- **AREAS AROUND ELECTRICAL OR CABLE WIRING, VENTS, AND PIPES.** Seal the smaller areas with caulk, and for anything bigger than a couple of inches, use spray foam.

- **DUCTWORK.** Leakage thought the ductwork makes your cooling or heating system work harder and wastes energy and money. It can help to wrap ducts with insulation. To plug leaks, tape ducts with metallic or mastic tape. (Surprisingly, duct tape really isn't ideal for ducts.)

"You know you have perfection of design not when you have nothing more to add, but when you have nothing more to take away."

—Antoine de Saint Exupéry, author

SMARTER ROOFS

   You may not think your roof does much more than shelter you from the elements, but today's roofs have environmentally friendly powers that you may not know about.

- **COOL ROOFS:** Made with reflective materials, cool roofs are designed to reflect the sun's heat away from the house, lowering the roof temperature dramatically and reducing the energy needed to cool the home.

- **PLANET-FRIENDLY MATERIALS:** Many companies make roofing materials from recycled rubber or plastic that look like wooden shingles; you may also be able to find salvaged roofing materials, such as slate.

- **GREEN ROOFING:** A green roof is a multilayered system of insulation, waterproofing, root barriers, drainage, and lightweight soil, all topped with plants. A green roof provides insulation, protects your roof from the elements, filters pollutants from the air and rainwater, and provides habitat for wildlife. Even if you use conventional roofing materials such as asphalt shingles, it pays to choose the most durable materials; a long-lasting roof that does not need to be replaced uses fewer resources.

CHECK YOUR GARAGE DOOR SEAL

 For those homes with attached garages, an overlooked energy-robber is the garage door. If the door isn't properly sealed, it can allow heat to escape during winter and let cold air out during the summer. What may be worse, though, is that a leaky garage door can also be a health hazard, allowing toxic car emissions into your house.

Start by taking a close look around all the edges of the door to your garage—don't forget the bottom and top—and if you can see light shining through, use some weather stripping to seal the openings.

GREEN FACT... The Energy Star rating system is used throughout the world.

Although the Energy Star system of rating appliances and other electronic devices originated in the United States, it's now used throughout the world, including the European Union, Australia, Canada, Japan, New Zealand, and Taiwan. An appliance or electronic gadget with an Energy Star rating means it saves 20 to 30 percent more energy than required by federal standards.

BRIGHT IDEA: SOLAR POWER

 With recent innovations in solar panels, it makes more sense than ever to consider installing them on your home. The biggest plus: this source of power doesn't emit carbon dioxide or other pollutants. Fortunately, an increasing solar panel market has helped lower prices along with government incentive programs.

So, is your home right for a solar panel system? Take a look at this checklist and see:

- **SHADE-FREE ROOF.** It doesn't matter where you live, as long as there is a non-shaded exposure on your roof, solar power can be an option. For example, if you live in the northern hemisphere as long as the roof faces south, east, or west, you'll have enough sun for solar panels.

- **ENOUGH SPACE.** To provide enough power for a home, a solar panel system would need to generate 3 to 6 kilowatts of power. Each kilowatt requires about 100 square feet (30 sq. m) of panels. That means you'd need about 300 to 600 square feet (91 to 182 sq. m) worth of space on your roof.

- **LIFE LEFT IN ROOF.** Most solar panel systems have a lifespan of decades—often about 30 years. So, the roof underneath should be in decent condition to avoid having to remove the panels soon after they're placed.

AN OVERLOOKED ENERGY WASTER: EXTERIOR LIGHTS

  Porch and other outdoor lights are important safety features. If kept on all night or during the day, however, that's a major waste. So it's important to upgrade them to more energy-efficient alternatives.

Walk around the outside of your home and decide whether compact fluorescent lightbulbs or LEDs would serve your outdoor fixtures best. Consider installing motion detectors that illuminate your home or yard only when needed; many detectors can also sense daylight and will turn off the lights when not needed.

GREEN FACT... Opening the oven door while cooking wastes energy and lengthens cooking time.

When you open the oven door while baking, the temperature can drop by as much as 25 ° (14 ° C). That means the oven will need to bump up the temperature to resume baking at the desired temperature. Don't check unnecessarily.

Green Family 101:
SWITCHING TO ENERGY-EFFICIENT LIGHTBULBS

The facts are incontrovertible: if every household in the United States replaced just one conventional, incandescent lightbulb with a compact fluorescent lightbulb (CFL), the annual energy savings would amount to more than $600 million and it would avoid the equivalent of 800,000 cars' worth of greenhouse gas emissions. Yet many people are confused about making the switch or reluctant to do so because the quality of light seems less appealing. So what's a green family to do? Let me shed a little light on the situation!

There are actually two kinds of energy-efficient lightbulbs that are replacing old-fashioned incandescents: the above-mentioned CFLs and the even more efficient LED (light-emitting diode) bulbs. CFLs use much less energy to produce the same amount of light as incandescents, do not lose heat the way incandescents do, and last much longer. The new LEDs, which are not yet widely available but are becoming more common, last as much as 10 times longer than the CFLs. When you first make the switch, you'll probably be choosing CFLs.

The trick to avoiding the harsh, overly bright light that many people associate with energy-efficient bulbs is to pay attention not to the watts, which actually measure the energy output of the bulb, but to the Kelvin rating, which gives you a better sense of the color. For warmer color, look for 2700 to 3000K, and a label that says "soft white" or "warm glow." The higher Kelvin bulbs, 3500 to 4100K, give off a bright white light, while those at 5000 to 6500K are bluer and most like daylight. The chart below summarizes what you need to know about energy-efficient bulbs.

	DIMMER • • • • • • • • • • • BRIGHTER			
Lumens	450	800	1100	1600
Standard Incandescent	40w	60w	75w	100w
Halogen Incadescents	29w	43w	53w	72w
CFLs	9w	14w	19w	23w
LEDs	8w	13w	17w	N/A

Green Family 101:
REMODELING WITH RECYCLING

When you remodel, not only do you have the chance to freshen paint or add another bathroom, you have the opportunity to incorporate earth-friendly ideas to help you save money, reduce heating and cooling needs, and increase durability.

- **SEEK OUT RECYCLED-CONTENT MATERIALS.** Many products are now made of recycled materials. Kitchen countertops for example, are made from recycled stone, glass, and paper.

- **USE LOW-VOC PAINTS, COATINGS, AND SEALANTS.** Conventional caulk, paint, and flooring adhesives often contain volatile organic compounds (VOCs). One example of these compounds is formaldehyde, which can trigger allergies and asthma. Chose only low- or no-VOC forumulas.

- **LOOK USED BEFORE BUYING NEW.** Whether it's a kitchen sink or bathtub, check out green building sources and architectural salvage and supply stores, both online and off.

- **DETERMINE DURABILITY.** By opting for the more-durable products, you'll save money in the long run. One such example: replacing vinyl flooring with natural linoleum.

• **ADD INSULATION WHENEVER POSSIBLE.** Whether you have stripped the walls to the studs or you're just patching a hole in a wall, take the opportunity to put in new insulation. One good, green option is dense-pack cellulose, which is made from recycled newspaper.

Let your contractor know you're serious about a green renovation. Perhaps that new bamboo flooring for your kitchen has been sustainably harvested—but if it traveled halfway across the world to your kitchen floor, a lot of resources were used in transportation. Here are seven questions to ask contractors and building suppliers before your renovation:

[ ] Have you had experience with green renovations?

[ ] Is the wood used in the project certified as sustainably harvested?

[ ] How difficult will the flooring be to maintain?

[ ] What will be done with any old materials from the renovation?

[ ] Can the green requirements for the project be written into the contract?

[ ] What are the considerations for indoor air quality related to the project?

[ ] Are there more energy-efficient options for fixtures or appliances?

CHAPTER FIVE

Lawn & Garden

Your lawn and garden are lush and growing—but are they truly green? Traditional landscaping practices can often have negative impacts on the environment. Gardening with toxic chemicals such as pesticides and herbicides contaminates soil, air, and water. Gas-powered equipment is polluting and noisy. Fortunately, there are lots of ways to grow your garden and maintain your yard without resorting to such practices; in fact, you can make yard and garden choices that will actually benefit the soil, water, and air around you. Green gardening requires 3 main strategies: conserving water and soil, following organic practices, and controlling invasive species. In this chapter, you will find lots of great tips to help you grow a healthy, beautiful garden and make your landscape truly green.

> "The glory of gardening: hands in the dirt, head in the sun, heart with nature. To nurture a garden is to feed not just on the body, but the soul."
>
> **—Alfred Austin, English poet laureate**

IS YOUR WATER RUNNING? BETTER CATCH IT

  Every time you open your water bill, you realize that water is a precious resource. Especially in warmer climates and during warm months, the extra amount of water you use in your yard is likely to be reflected in your water bill. According to the U.S. EPA, some 30 percent of American homeowners' water use is devoted to outdoor spaces. How can you use just enough but not too much water and still keep your yard green? Start with sensible landscape planning to avoid excessive water use and waste.

Be sure that the ground around your house slopes downward at 1 percent or more.

Reduce the amount of turf (conventional grass lawn).

Add porous walkways and gravel trenches along driveways or patios to collect water.

Clean storm gutters at least twice a year, more in the fall if clogged by leaves, and add a rain barrel to collect roof runoff—then use the water in your garden.

TOSS THE TURF

The traditional grass lawn is not sustainable. It requires a lot of water but has a much lower water retention capacity than a meadow, woodland, or other more natural, less manicured habitat. To retain the look of the classic green carpet, a turf lawn needs regular mowing, fertilizing, and weeding, which typically leads to the use of power mowers and chemicals. For a greener yard, reduce the amount of turf grass by half—or all together!

Some alternatives include:

- Create an alternative "lawn" with native grasses or low-growing plants such as groundcovers, or in shady spots, moss

- Extend garden beds into areas formerly used for grass

- Add patios, walkways, or decking

"Knowing trees, I understand the meaning of patience. Knowing grass, I can appreciate persistence."
—Hal Borland, author and environmental columnist for *The New York Times*

WATER WISELY

  Most established gardens prefer deep, infrequent watering as opposed to frequent surface watering; the former creates healthy root systems, while the latter leads to shallow roots and increased evaporation. (This does not apply to new plantings.) A great way to avoid wasteful overwatering is to practice sensible watering techniques:

- **WATER THE SOIL, NOT THE LEAVES.** Instead of spraying your plants all over, use a water-breaker nozzle at the end of your hose and aim at the plants' root area so the soil can drink deeply.

- **WATER IN THE EARLY MORNING BEFORE THE SUN IS HIGH.** If your plants are thoroughly watered early in the day, they can better withstand the heat and sun of midday. If you wait, the sun will evaporate the water very quickly.

- **IF YOU HAVE TO WATER LATER, WAIT UNTIL LATE AFTERNOON.** Later in the day is a good time to water as well, but do not water in the evening, as the plants need time to dry to avoid growth of fungi.

RETAIN WATER WITH MULCH

 When there's a layer of mulch on top of your garden, it helps lock in moisture that would otherwise evaporate, reduces the weed population, and enriches your soil. During cold seasons, it can protect more delicate plants from freezing temperatures. In hot weather, it can help keep the soil cool. There are lots of mulching materials, including leaf mulch (shredded leaves), pine bark, hardwood bark, grass clippings and yard waste, compost, gravel, straw, coconut fibers, and even mulching fabrics. Your local municipality may offer free mulch. Check with your local garden center or research online to find out the right mulch for your plants, and follow these guidelines when applying:

- Weed before you mulch

- For new beds, apply mulch to a depth of 3 to 6 inches (7.5 to 15 cm)

- For established beds, 2 to 3 inches (5 to 7.5 cm) is usually plenty

- Leave some space around the base of each plant so air can circulate

- Keep your mulch layer intact, adding more as needed to prevent any bare spots

- Avoid cocoa shell mulch, which can be toxic to pets

USE WATER-WISE IRRIGATION METHODS

 Many gardeners water by hand with a hose or set up a sprinkler and let it run, but there are more water-wise and time-efficient methods that will deliver water directly to your plants and save you time.

USE A SOAKER HOSE. Instead of spraying and wasting lots of water, lay a soaker hose. These hoses use up to 70 percent less water than a sprinkler but still provide water to plants where they need it the most.

INSTALL A DRIP IRRIGATION SYSTEM. A system of tubes and valves, a drip irrigation system delivers the right amount of water to each plant. You can attach a timer, as well.

ATTACH A WEATHER SENSOR TO YOUR TIMER. These handy gadgets shut off the system when watering is not appropriate, such as when it rains, freezes, or is extremely windy.

USE A RAIN BARREL. Attached to your home's downspout, a rain barrel collects the runoff from your roof when it rains. You can then harvest the rainwater for your plants or connect it directly to your irrigation system.

CHECK HOSES. Maintain your equipment, fix drips and leaks, and replace as soon as needed.

PLANT A XERISCAPE GARDEN

 A fancy term for low-water gardening, xeriscaping means choosing plants for your garden that do not require much, if any, supplemental watering. By reducing or eliminating the need to add water beyond what nature provides, you are making a huge difference in terms of water and resource usage. Although xeriscaping originated for use in dry, drought-prone climates, its water-friendly approach has made it popular everywhere people are concerned about the environment, and it works in any region. To get started, you'll need a good sense of the rainfall in your region and a solid understanding of the micorclimate and soil types in your garden or yard.

The main elements of planting a xeriscape:

MAKE SURE YOUR SOIL HOLDS WATER AS WELL AS IT CAN but also drains properly. The trick is to add organic material—that's compost!—and to keep the soil well-aerated by turning it before you plant.

KNOW YOUR EXPOSURES. For the areas of your yard that face south and west, and therefore get the most sun, use plants that need only a minimum of water. In spots that are north- and east-facing, you can choose plants that like more moisture. Don't mix plants with high- and low-watering needs in the same planting area.

SELECT DROUGHT-TOLERANT, NATIVE PLANTS THAT HAVE LOW-WATER NEEDS. Native, or indigenous, plants are those that grow naturally in your region. That means they are naturally adapted to grow with the amount of moisture readily available in the landscape. Native species tend to be hardier and more disease and pest resistant than non-natives. They require little maintenance and often provide habitat and food for local birds and other wildlife.

CHOOSE LOW-WATER GRASSES OR GROUNDCOVERS TO REPLACE TURF. Look for native species that can replace thirsty turf grasses. Your local garden center is a great resource for finding natives.

MULCH. What can't it do? Mulching helps your soil retain its moisture, prevents its erosion, and improves its quality.

GREEN FACT...Less than 10 percent of insects are harmful to plants.

This means using harsh chemical insecticides is extreme overkill. And you may be getting rid of beneficial insects instead of targeting the ones truly causing damage to any plants. Pesticides can also run off into water supplies, causing damage to aquatic life.

Green Family 101:
COMPOSTING: PART 1

Composting is, hands-down, one of the best ways to transform waste into something useful. Indeed, compost—which can be used both for amending soil and for mulching—is a material so beneficial to soil that gardeners often call it "black gold." Composting means that you're creating an optimal environment for waste materials (such as kitchen scraps, old newspapers, and yard waste) to naturally decompose.

What's better: It's easy for kids to help by collecting and putting in materials, turning the compost, and harvesting it when it's "cooked."

If you have lots of yard space and a discreet corner, you may choose to go binless; if you have less room or want to keep it fully contained, opt for a bin. Here's what you need to know to get started:

- **For binless composting, choose a discreet place in your yard away from your house and other buildings.** Pick a dry spot with partial sun—compost decomposes fastest between 120° and 160° F (48-70° C). But don't worry if your spot is cooler. With good aeration and moisture, and the right ingredient mix, your compost will continue to decompose at temperatures of 50° F (10° C) or above. Below that, it will go dormant until the weather warms up.

- **No yard? You can still compost.** Kitchen composting, with or without worms (See pages 22–23) is a great option for those without the right outdoor space.

- **If you want to keep your compost in a bin, make or buy one.** Purchase an enclosed compost bin or tumbler. There are many options available that are designed to save time and space. If you go the DIY route, make sure your box is at least 3 x 3 x 3 feet (.75 cubic m) in size.

- **Balance materials.** The microbes responsible for breaking down your materials need a balanced diet of nitrogen and carbon. Nitrogen comes from green materials such as food scraps and grass clippings. Carbon comes from brown materials such as dead leaves, wood chips, and shredded newspaper. A ratio that contains equal portions by weight (not volume) of both works best. (See page 124–125 for a detailed list of what to put in your compost.)

- **Add air and water.** In addition to green and brown materials, compost requires air and water. Add air by turning your compost regularly—either with a rake or by turning your bin. Keep it moist with extra water, if needed—the optimum microbial habitat is achieved when the pile is about as moist as a wrung-out sponge.

- **Don't squish.** When adding organic matter to your compost, don't press the materials down to make more space. You will squeeze out the air that microbes in the compost pile need.

USE PUSH POWER

 Get rid of your power gardening tools—the gas-powered mower, weed whacker, edge trimmer, and leaf blower. But wait, you say, the engines on mowers, chain saws, snow blowers, and other outdoor equipment are small and don't really emit too much pollution, right? Unfortunately, wrong. These small engines pump out a host of pollutants, including hydrocarbons, nitrogen oxides, and carbon monoxide. These gases contribute to acid rain and smog and can irritate lungs and restrict plant growth. Go manual, and you'll improve the air quality immediately—and maybe your health, too, as push-power is better for your body as well as the planet.

LET THE GRASS GROW

 To keep the lawn you do have from turning brown during the hottest days, simply raise the height of your mower by a half an inch to an inch (about 1cm to 2.5cm). Cutting the grass too short during the summer can damage the grass and promote weed growth.

The longer grass helps keep the roots shaded, cooler, and better able to retain moisture. Also, allow grass clippings to stay on your lawn. They provide nutrients and shade, too. And know that during the hottest periods, if your lawn browns, it is just going dormant—not dead—and will come back to green life when the rain begins again.

TRIM THE ENVIRONMENTAL IMPACT
OF MOWERS

  The best thing to do is use a manual mower, but if you cannot make the switch, follow these guidelines to minimize the environmental impact of your machines:

- **KEEP THEM IN TOP FORM.** By keeping these engines running at maximum efficiency, you're reducing the amount of pollution they produce. Change the oil and filters as per the manufacturers' recommendations.

- **USE A FUNNEL FOR FUEL.** Spilling gasoline pollutes the environment. In addition to spoiling the ground, the fumes contribute to air pollution.

- **CLEAN AND SHARPEN BLADES.** Dull blades and a mowing deck clogged with grass make your mower inefficient, and dull blades make grass more prone to disease. Sharpen them at least once a year, ideally in the spring.

- **UPGRADE AND RECYCLE.** Increasingly, mowing and lawn equipment manufacturers are addressing environmental concerns. Newer equipment is being made that's more efficient and has lower emissions or is electric instead of gas-powered. But don't just toss your old mower. Take it to a recycling center, where the parts can be converted to raw materials.

BANISH THE 'CIDES

 Take a look inside your garden shed: do the shelves contain pesticides, fungicides, and herbicides, all marked with prominent safety warnings? If so, you'll want to make eliminating those toxic-chemical-laden products a priority in your plan for going green in the garden. Organic, natural alternatives exist for almost every situation in your garden from pests to diseases. Here's how to have a flourishing garden without the 'cides.

- **PREVENTION.** Choose native plants, which are naturally more pest- and disease-resistant, and be vigilant about keeping them healthy.

- **AGGRESSION.** You can manually remove many pests as soon as you see them. Aphids can be wiped off with a wet cloth dipped in soapy water. Unwelcome caterpillars can be plucked from plants with a gloved hand and deposited in your bucket of soapy water.

- **ROTATION.** Putting the same plants in the same spots year after year makes it easier for pests and diseases to return. Rotate your plants to different locations.

- **COMPANIONSHIP.** Mix up your beds to include some plants that naturally repel pests and others that attract good bugs. For example, borage repels tomato hornworms but attracts bees.

CONTROL INVADERS WITHOUT CHEMICALS

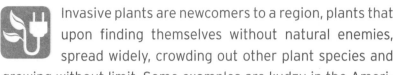 Invasive plants are newcomers to a region, plants that upon finding themselves without natural enemies, spread widely, crowding out other plant species and growing without limit. Some examples are kudzu in the American South or purple loosestrife in the northwestern United States and British Columbia. Familiarize yourself with the common invaders in your region, and don't plant them. Vigilance is the key to keeping these plants out of your yard—as soon as you see them, eliminate them. Mechanical removal—digging them up—is the greenest way to remove the invaders from your yard, but it can be a long process, requiring careful removal of all the pieces, as these tough plants often resprout. Application of vinegar may help, but even the most eco-consious gardeners sometimes must resort to targeted, careful use of glyphosate to get rid of the invaders for good.

"Every blade of grass has its angel that bends and whispers, 'Grow, grow.'"

—The Talmud

6 NATURAL WAYS TO RID YOUR LAWN OF DANDELIONS

The yellow flowers of dandelions dotting your lawn are a cheerful sight–unless you consider dandelions unwelcome visitors, in which case you need a solution for ridding your lawn of them. There's no reason to reach for harsh chemical herbicides to tame the dandelion hordes. Instead, these six natural solutions can give you a green lawn:

- **MOW OFTEN AND HIGH.** Make your mower do the work by buzzing off the yellow flowering tops before they morph into seeds and fly off. Keep your grass trimmed fairly high–about 2.5 inches (a little more than 6 cm). Shorter grass promotes dandelion growth.

- **BOIL 'EM.** If only a few of the plants are poking up in your lawn, a good elimination method is drench them in boiling water.

- **MULCH 'EM.** When dandelions encroach on gardens, mulch can smother them. First lay down a layer of cardboard or plastic sheeting, then add mulch.

- **SQUIRT SOME VINEGAR.** When you first see dandelion plants sprouting up, give them a spritz of white or apple cider vinegar directly on the stems. However, be aware that vinegar can also kill grass.

- **BOOST SOIL QUALITY.** A higher-quality mixture of compost and mulch will make the area less hospitable to weeds, which grow well in acidic, poor-quality soils. Another benefit: The soil will benefit the plants you want to flourish.

- **SPREAD CORN GLUTEN MEAL.** About four to six weeks before the dandelions germinate, spread corn gluten meal (available at garden centers) over the area. The good news: corn gluten meal doesn't affect other plants, like grass, that are already in place.

GREEN FACT... About 1 hour of lawn mowing equals 100 miles of pollution from a car.

The *putt-putt* from a lawn mower can do more damage to the environment than you may think. Mowers also produce pollutants called polycyclic aromatic hydrocarbons. Unlike cars, these engines don't have catalytic converters; however, if catalytic converters were installed on mowers, more than 80 percent of pollutants would be reduced.

BUST BLACK SPOT FUNGUS WITH A SIMPLE SOLUTION

 One of the banes of any rose gardener is black spot. The nasty fungus leaves spots on rosebush leaves and can ruin the plant, even killing it. Fortunately, all you need to guard against this ugly invader is probably already in your pantry.

---

2 QUARTS (2 L) WARM WATER

1 1/2 TEASPOONS (7 G) BAKING SODA

1/2 TEASPOON (2.5 ML) DISH SOAP

SPRAY BOTTLE

Mix the ingredients together and pour into spray bottle. Spritz the formula on leaves once a week during the morning.

"A lawn is nature under totalitarian rule."

—Michael Pollan, author of *The Omnivore's Dilemma*

ELIMINATE POISON IVY WITHOUT HARSH CHEMICALS

 One of the most unwelcome visitors to any yard is poison ivy, which causes a nasty rash when it comes into contact with your skin. Some people have very severe reactions, and if you happen to accidentally burn some of the stuff, the smoke could dangerously inflame air passages.

A simple formula can rid your yard of this plant without the use of harsh chemicals:

---

2 QUARTS (ABOUT 2 L) SOAPY WATER

1/2 CUP (150 G) SALT

SPRAY BOTTLE

Pour the soapy water into the bottle. Add salt and stir until the salt is completely dissolved. Spray the mixtures on leaves and stem. Be careful to direct your spray specifically to the poison ivy plant because this mixture will kill many other plants, not just poison ivy. Once the poison ivy is dead, use gloves to remove it and be careful not to touch the leaves, because their oil may still cause irritation.

NATURALLY BANISH CRABGRASS FROM YOUR LAWN

  Some folks joke that if you sit in a yard you can hear crabgrass growing. Crabgrass is tenacious. A single plant can produce 150,000 seeds. Once it gets hold in your lawn, it's one of the most notoriously difficult plants to get out. And pouring chemicals to stop it may cause damage to your lawn and the environment.

Take the natural solution. First, spray the area with a fine mist. It should be moist, not soaked. Pour about a 1/2 cup (110g) of baking soda in a sock, then tap the sock over the area of crabgrass. Within a day, the baking soda should cause the crabgrass to shrivel. What's even better: The surrounding grass isn't affected.

GREEN FACT... Trees can save energy costs.

When trees are positioned to shield your house from the sun, your energy consumption can be reduced by up to 25 percent. Such trees can reduce the typical daytime temperature of a house by 3° to 6° compared to a house in an area without trees.

PREVENT PESTS

 The easiest and cheapest way to avoid pest damage to your garden is to prevent them from coming in the first place. How can you keep the pests out? Try these tips:

- **CLEAN YOUR TOOLS.** Always disinfect at the start of the season and if you've been working with diseased plants.

- **IMPROVE YOUR SOIL.** Add compost, seaweed mulch, and use natural fertilizer as needed to keep your soil healthy.

- **ROTATE AND MIX PLANTS.** Pests tend to be plant-specific; moving the plants around from year to year and mixing in different species will help to make your plants less vulnerable to pests, and less likely to suffer a wide infestation.

- **WATER IN THE MORNING.** Wet foliage encourages fungal infections and insect damage.

- **REMOVE UNHEALTHY PLANTS QUICKLY.** Pests weaken plants and are attracted to weak plants. Remove them and dispose of them away from your garden.

REPEL STINGING INSECTS

   If your outdoor time is being ruined by the attacks of mosquitoes and other stinging insects, don't despair: Chances are your pantry contains many of the simple ingredients needed to make all-natural insect repellents. That means you don't need to swing around one of those bug-zapping tennis racquets like a crazed Roger Federer.

LEMON PEELS

The next time you're outside with guests, set out a bowl of lemon peels. Pinch the peel to squeeze out some of the essential lemon oil, then rub it on your skin.

VINEGAR

Pour some white or cider vinegar on a towel and lightly rub it on your skin. The acidic content of this stuff makes you less noticeable to insects.

GET BUGGY, IN A GOOD WAY

  Long before expensive chemicals were used to spray crops, nature had a way of taking care of pests: other insects. Here's your guide (opposite page) to which bugs you should get friendly with and how to invite them over to dine on your unwelcome garden pests.

BUG BUDDIES	PESTS THEY EAT	INVITE THEM
GROUND BEETLES	Cut worms, root maggots, slugs, snails, and other ground-based bugs	Provide ground cover such as mulch, branches, or stones
HOVER FLIES	The larvae devour aphids and other soft-bodied pests	Put out bright flowers that have pollen for adult hover flies to feed on
LACEWINGS	The larva of these fairy-like bugs eat aphids, caterpillars, and many others	Plant flowering plants that produce nectar
LADYBUGS	Aphids and other soft-bellied insects	Surround garden with flowering plants that produce nectar and pollen
PARASITIC WASPS	Larvae seeks out caterpillars, including corn earworm, tomato fruitworm, and cabbage worm	Flowering plants that produce pollen and nectar draw the adults
PIRATE BUGS	Tomato hornworms, spider mites, leafhopper nymphs, corn earworms, and others	Plant willows, buckwheat, corn, and flowering plants with nectar and pollen
SPIDERS	The terminators of the insect world, spiders will munch just about anything	Plant perennials and place straw and mulches around the garden

Green Family 101:
COMPOSTING: PART 2

Now that you're composting, you'll want to know what to put (and not to put) in. Compost materials can be divided into "green," which are high in nitrogen, and "brown," which are high in carbon. A good mix of the two will help your microbes to "cook" quickly. Consult this handy chart:

DO NOT ADD TO YOUR COMPOST	
meat and bones	may smell bad and attract vermin
poultry and fish	may smell bad and attract vermin
fatty or greasy food waste or dairy products	slow to decompose, may smell bad
invasive plants or noxious weeds	can grow and spread
glossy or colored paper	inks may contain heavy metals
dryer lint	may contain synthetic materials that won't decompose
pressure treated wood	contains chemicals
human or animal feces or pet litter	may carry disease

ADD TO YOUR COMPOST	
fruit and vegetable scraps N	bury them in the middle of the pile
eggshells N	best when crushed
food scraps N	bury these in the pile
coffee grounds N	you can even add the filters
tea leaves N	loose or in bags
grass clippings N **or garden waste**	only if grass isn't treated with chemicals
flowers, cuttings N	chop up woody stems
seaweed, algae, and kelp N	apply in thin layers
pine needles C	acidic; decompose slowly
newspaper C	do not use glossy or colored paper
cardboard C	shred
corncobs, stalks C	chop
sawdust C	add in layers
wood chips / pellets C	use sparingly

N = Nitrogen   C = Carbon

EUCALYPTIZE APHIDS

 Try this formula to get rid of aphids, bee-tles, earwigs, and slugs, especially on plants such as tomatoes, cucumbers, strawberries, and roses. You'll need:

---

2 CUPS (475 ML) WATER

2 TEASPOONS (10 ML) CANOLA OIL

1/2 TEASPOON (3 ML) EUCALYPTUS ESSENTIAL OIL

1/4 TEASPOON (1 ML) LIQUID CASTILE SOAP

---

1. In a large spray bottle, combine all the ingredients and shake until well blended.

2. As soon as you see any of the insects, spray the formula extensively on the plants and continue spraying about every three days until pests are gone. Don't store; for highest potency make a fresh batch before every application.

> "I believe a leaf of grass is no less than the journey-work of the stars."
>
> **–Walt Whitman, poet and author of *Leaves of Grass***

GET 'EM WITH GARLIC-PEPPER SPRAY

  Effective against aphids, cabbage worms, caterpillars, flea beetles, hornworms, and several others. You'll need:

---

1 HEAD GARLIC

1 LARGE ONION

2 TABLESPOONS (30 ML) DRIED RED PEPPER FLAKES

1 CUP (240 ML) WATER

1 TEASPOON (5 ML) LIQUID CASTILE SOAP

32-OUNCE (950 ML) SPRAY BOTTLE

---

1. Peel and roughly chop the garlic cloves and coarsely chop the onion.

2. Mix garlic, onion, and red pepper flakes in a food processor, slowly adding water.

3. Pour into a gallon jug and put in the refrigerator for a few days.

4. Using a strainer, pour 1 cup (240ml) into the spray bottle and fill the rest of the bottle with water.

5. Spray directly on affected plants. Wash hands after use and store in fridge.

SAY GOOD-BYE TO CABBAGE WORMS

  Cabbage worms gobble up not just your cabbages, but cauliflower, broccoli, radishes, kale, and other garden favorites. Fight back with this mixture. You'll need:

---

1 CUP (125 G) FLOUR

1/2 CUP (150 G) SALT

---

1. In a container such as a large salt shaker or a clean, used Parmesan cheese shaker, thoroughly mix the flour and salt.

2. During mornings or evenings when there is still dew on the plants, shake the mixture over the plants.

"I like it when a flower or a little tuft of grass grows through a crack in the concrete. It's so $@#%ing heroic."

—George Carlin, comedian

TRY AN INSECTICIDAL SOAP

  This formula of lemon and baby shampoo may seem innocent to you but it's anathema to aphids. You'll need:

2 CUPS (500 ML) WATER

1 TABLESPOON (15 ML) LEMON JUICE

1 TABLESPOON (15 ML) BABY SHAMPOO

1. In a spray bottle, combine all the ingredients until well blended.
2. Early in the morning, spray on areas where aphids are present. Continue to apply until you see no signs of the aphids.

KILL SLUGS WITH SALT

  Slugs can devastate a garden, but a great defense agains slugs is plain old table salt. You'll need:

SALT

SHAKER

In the morning, head out and inspect your garden, looking for slugs on plants. A few shakes directly on the slug will do the trick.

NATURAL SOLUTIONS TO DEER TROUBLES

Bambi sure looks cute in the movies. But when the deer are munching the pepper plants in your garden, they're decidedly much less appealing. It's enough to make you think about serving venison! Before you get violent, consider some natural deterrents.

UNAPPEALING FOODS. Start by planting some vegetation that deer don't enjoy nibbling, such as plants with thick leaves, those with minty or lemon scents, and prickly vines.

CREATE A NATURAL BARRIER. Use plants that deer don't like to create natural barriers around your garden. Some to try include butterfly bush, buttonbush, coralberry, dogwood, and elderberry. Sunflowers, Jerusalem artichokes, switchgrass, and thorny gooseberries can also assist in repelling deer.

FENCE THEM OUT. If the deer infestation is significant, you may simply have to put up a mesh fence. Make it doubly effective by planting deer-unfriendly plants within and around the fence.

REUSE LEAVES FOR MULCH

The changing of the season and falling leaves provides an opportunity to fertilize your lawn. Here's how to reuse your leaves for mulch:

1. Rake all your leaves together in one area and after you're done jumping in them, spread them so they're flat but still together.

2. Mow them repeatedly. All the leaves should be shredded. Mow over the area until you don't see any whole leaves in the bunch.

3. Collect the leaves and place them in a sealed bin. Unlike compost, you want to keep the mulch dry and avoid decomposition. Mulch will act to insulate the soil.

4. At the start of spring, evenly spread the leaf mulch over your garden. It will help keep moisture in the ground, and the leaves will eventually decompose and act as fertilizer, too.

"I KNOW THE PLEASURE OF PULLING UP ROOT VEGETABLES. THEY ARE SOLVABLE MYSTERIES."

–Novella Carpenter, author of *Farm City: The Education of an Urban Farmer*

GET THE DIRT ON ORGANIC FERTILIZERS

   For thriving lawns and gardens, fertilizers are essential. But the type of fertilizer you select may have a lasting impact on your growing success and the environment. Fertilizers provide nutrients to the soil and may make up for any nutritional imbalances present. There are two types of fertilizers: organic and inorganic.

Organic fertilizers include compost, animal manure, and plant-based meals. Inorganic fertilizers are composed of minerals or synthetic chemicals. Organic fertilizers bolster the soil over the long haul. Inorganic fertilizers may contain a higher percentage of nutrients and work more quickly, but they not only lack the longer-lasting, sustainable benefits of inorganic fertilizer, they may also leach chemicals into groundwater and runoff, causing serious environmental problems.

The organic stuff also helps encourage an environment that supports sustainable growth. For example, organic fertilizer supports the life cycle of earthworms. And because organic fertilizer slowly releases its nutrients into the ground, there's less risk of losing those nutrients for the following planting seasons, whereas inorganic fertilizer must be applied and re-applied year after year.

Follow these guidelines for applying fertilizer:

- **DON'T OVERDO IT.** For most lawns, once a year (usually in the fall) is enough to apply fertilizer. For gardens, apply only as needed depending on your particular plants.

- **TEST SOIL FIRST.** You can't make the right decision about fertilizer if you don't know what nutrients your soil needs.

- **GO SLOW ON SLOPES.** Especially if your lawn is sloped, use slow-release fertilizers. This avoids having nutrients washed away with rain.

- **KEEP AN EYE ON WEATHER.** Don't apply fertilizers before or during rain. You're just allowing the fertilizer to be immediately washed away before it has had a chance to work into the soil.

- **DIAL IN APPLICATOR.** Especially on older fertilizer applicators, you should check to see if the application settings are accurate. Carefully follow application instructions, too.

HOW TO USE COMPOST

 You've collected table scraps, added yard clippings, turned it, and now, some eight weeks later, you have a lovely pile of black stuff. What next? You know compost helps condition your lawn and garden by slowly releasing nutrients and improving moisture retention. But how do you actually use the stuff?

TEST your compost by putting a handful in a plastic bag for three days. Open the bag and if it smells like ammonia, your compost has some more cooking to do. Try again in another week.

Once it's ready to use, here's what you can do with it:

- **START SEEDS.** Use a mixture of about one-third sand and two-thirds compost to give your seeds a nutrient-rich environment in which to grow.

- **BLEND INTO GARDEN BEDS.** Before you plant, mix compost into the soil of your garden beds. Make sure to spread it evenly.

- **SPREAD OVER LAWN.** A thin layer of compost scattered over your lawn once or twice a year can promote healthy growth.

- **BLEND INTO POTTING SOIL.** Sift out larger chunks of compost with a screen, then mix about one part compost to two parts soil to make your own potting mix.

- **MULCH AND FERTILIZE.** Around the base of plants, add about 2 to 3 inches (5 to 7.5 cm) to the surrounding soil.

SPRINKLE, SPRINKLE

 To maintain the small patch of lawn you've decided to keep without too much guilt, try these water conservation tips:

- **SET SPRINKLERS TO WATER ONLY THE LAWN**, not the driveway, sidewalk, or other impervious surface where the water will be wasted.

- **WATER ONLY WHEN IT'S NEEDED.** Most lawns require about an inch (2.5 cm) per week. If it has rained or is going to rain, don't hand water your lawn.

- **USE ONLY AS MUCH WATER AS YOUR LAWN NEEDS.** Measure the amount of water coming from your sprinkler and from the rain with a can or rain gauge, and adjust your watering schedule accordingly.

CHAPTER SIX

Eco-Friendly Pets

RAISING ECO-FRIENDLY PETS

Pets are family, too. And, though you may never have thought about it, your pet does have a carbon footprint. How can you make pet ownership and care part of your green family strategy? By following many of the same principles in this book for conservation, recycling, using organic products, and repurposing, of course! This chapter offers plenty of tips for environmentally friendly pet care—mostly of dogs and cats, though you can apply these tricks to almost any pet, with a little bit of adjustment to your particular companion.

"A good deed done to an animal is as meritorious as a good deed done to a human being, while an act of cruelty to an animal is as bad as an act of cruelty to a human being."

—Mohammed

ADOPT OR RESCUE A PET

  Adopting a pet from a shelter or rescue center is a good deed, indeed. Each year, tens of thousands of unwanted pets end up at animal welfare centers, where, if they are not adopted, they are euthanized. You can help combat overpopulation and rescue an unwanted animal by choosing to get your pet from a shelter. Though many commercial breeders are responsible, some, sadly, are guilty of inbreeding, overbreeding, and subjecting animals to less-than-healthy conditions. Why risk supporting one of these unscrupulous breeders when you can easily adopt? Many reputable organizations exist that will help to arrange for your pet adoption, and most of them also provide neutering or spaying services and advice on caring for your new pet.

GREEN FACT... Indoor cats usually live at least twice as long as outdoor cats do.

Along with having your pet around for a long time, having an indoor cat means you more reliably dispose of waste. An outdoor cat will go just about anywhere outside—even in the neighbor's flower bed.

BELL THE CAT OR BAR THE DOORS

 One of the most serious dangers to the local bird population? Yes, it's sweet little Fluffy, a lethal weapon second only to habitat destruction. Put a bell on her collar—she'll still have the fun of stalking her prey, but the birds will be warned that she's coming.

Even safer, and not just for the birds, is to commit to keeping your kitty indoors. Vets say that indoor cats live longer, healthier lives.

MAKE THE KINDEST CUT

 Be a responsible pet owner by spaying or neutering your pet. You'll be keeping your pet healthier (neutered pets are at less risk for certain diseases) and doing a good turn for the environment as well. Spaying or neutering your pet helps to prevent overpopulation and will save another generation of unwanted kittens or puppies from a shelter.

And though it probably goes without saying, take your pet to the vet for regular check-ups and care. A healthy pet costs much less in resources and energy than a sick one.

SHOP GREEN

 When it's time to buy pet food and supplies, follow the same sustainable shopping strategies you use for the rest of the family:

- **BUY ORGANIC.** Look for organic pet food brands, and read labels to be sure you're getting the real thing rather than a "greenwashed" brand. Natural and organic brands make pet food with sustainably and humanely raised meats and without added drugs or hormones. Similarly, when it's time to purchase pet care products such as shampoo, choose the organic, natural products whenever possible.

- **OPT FOR RECYCLED.** As the green movement has grown, the pet category has expanded to include many more environmentally friendly products, such as toys and bedding products made with recycled or sustainably produced content, natural materials (such as hemp), and minimal packaging.

"Our pets are our family."

—Ana Monnar, author

THINK GLOBAL, BARK LOCAL

 Just like with your food chain, the closer the origin of your pet's food, the less impact its production has on the environment. Just like you, your pet should be a locavore.

Instead of buying food that's shipped across the country, look for brands that are made near you. Many farmers' markets have vendors that specialize in natural, organic animal food that's grown nearby.

GREEN FACT... Even if you don't want to own a pet, you can adopt an animal and help preserve its habitat.

Perhaps allergies have kept you from adopting a furry friend. Or maybe you live somewhere that does not allow pets. You can still "adopt" an animal by making a donation to organizations that preserve wildlife habitats. Some organizations may give donors a stuffed toy that resembles their adopted animal. Check out these organizations: Friend a Gorilla, Red Panda Network, Whale or Dolphin Conservation Society, and Defenders of Wildlife.

MAKE YOUR OWN DOG TREATS

  Making your own dog treats not only lowers your carbon footprint and use of packaging but also reduces your grocery bill! Here's one recipe for treats that are sure to get tails wagging:

---

1 CUP (220 G) WHOLE WHEAT FLOUR, PLUS ADDITIONAL FLOUR FOR ROLLING

1/3 CUP (75 G) CORNMEAL

1 TABLESPOON (15 ML) VEGETABLE OIL

1/4 CUP (60 ML) LOW-SODIUM CHICKEN BROTH

1 EGG

2 TABLESPOONS (30 ML) MILK

---

1. Preheat oven to 350F. Line a baking sheet with parchment and set aside.

2. Combine the flour and cornmeal in a large bowl. Add the oil, broth, egg, and milk. Stir until a stiff dough forms.

3. Transfer mixture to a lightly floured surface. Pat dough into a disc shape and roll to 1/4" (6.25 mm) thickness.

4. Cut into 1" (2.5 cm) squares and transfer to prepared baking sheet.

5. Bake squares for 20 minutes or until lightly browned. Let cool and then store in a tightly sealed container.

MAKE YOUR OWN PET FOOD

 Find out from your veterinarian whether you can make your pet's food from scratch. Cats and dogs each require a specific combination of nutrients, and your particular animal may need something special depending on its breed, condition, and age. But just as with people, a meal of nutritionally balanced, homemade food is much healthier than pet food from a can or bag. Your vet may have recipes to recommend, or you can find several books and online resources with easy recipes for making homemade pet food.

POOP AND SCOOP

 One of the most important things you can do to help the environment as a dog owner is to pick up after Fido. Leaving the poop where it was deposited is not only unpleasant and inconsiderate, it can lead to contaminated groundwater and soil as the excrement releases disease-carrying bacteria and parasites. Bag your dog's doo-doo with a compostable or biodegradable plastic bag and dispose of it properly.

MIX SOME EARTH-FRIENDLY CAT LITTER

  You're bound to go through a lot of kitty litter during the lifetime of your cat, so why not make it an earth-friendly variety? Many commercial cat litters contain ingredients that are problematic, such as sodium bentonite (a type of clay that is strip-mined). Look for litter made from corn, wheat, wood chips, or even recycled newspaper. If you're feeling the DIY urge, you can even make your own:

---

8 SHEETS OF OLD NEWSPAPER

1 CUP (220G) BICARBONATE OF SODA

4 DROPS BIODEGRADABLE DISH SOAP

---

1. Shred newspaper into thin strips. You can use a shredder or simply tear into strips.

2. Add 4 drops of dish soap to a bucket of warm water. Soak the shredded paper in the bucket. Drain the water, then rinse the paper. Much of the ink will wash out. Drain thoroughly using a colander; use your hands to squeeze out as much water as possible.

3. Sprinkle with the bicarbonate of soda.

4. Crumble the newspaper into small clumps, and spread across a screen or sheet for drying. Put it out in the sun to help speed drying. When it is dry, use your homemade cat litter just like a commercial litter.

HOW TO ELIMINATE CAT BOX ODOR

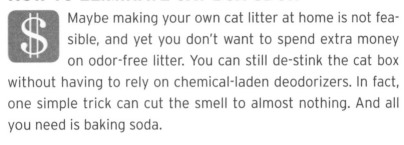 Maybe making your own cat litter at home is not feasible, and yet you don't want to spend extra money on odor-free litter. You can still de-stink the cat box without having to rely on chemical-laden deodorizers. In fact, one simple trick can cut the smell to almost nothing. And all you need is baking soda.

---

1 CUP (220 G) BAKING SODA

---

1. Pour about half the amount of litter you would normally put into the box.

2. Evenly spread the baking soda over the top of the that initial layer.

3. Add another layer of litter and Mr. Snuggles will have a much nicer smelling box.

> "If you pick up a starving dog and make him prosperous, he will not bite you. It is the principal difference between a dog and a man."
>
> **—Mark Twain**

HOW TO WEIGH DIFFERENT LITTER OPTIONS

 Each of the different kinds of cat litter options has different effects on the environment. Here's a quick primer:

- **CLAY-BASED:** Least green. In addition to needing to be mined, clay also contributes to landfills.

- **SILICA:** Soaks up odor and doesn't need to be changed as often, but the silica dust may be harmful to cats' lungs.

- **PLANT-BASED:** Although the content of plant-based litter is more environmentally friendly, the used litter still takes up landfill space.

- **ECO-FRIENDLY:** There are a number of green cat litter products on the market, though you may have to search to find them. They utilize sawdust, wood chips or shavings, recycled newspaper, and even grains such as wheat or corn.

GREEN FACT... Pet litter pollutes.

About 2 million tons (1.9 million t) of kitty litter alone goes into U.S. landfills each year.

CAN ANIMAL WASTE BE FLUSHED?

 Dog feces can usually be flushed with no problem. (The trick, of course, is getting him to sit on the toilet.) However, cat poo, especially if it has been in litter, shouldn't be flushed down the toilet.

Litter can clog up plumbing systems and create water pollution. In addition, cat waste can carry *toxoplasma gondii*, a parasite that wastewater treatment facilities don't usually treat for. So, keep kitty away from the toilet bowl.

CAN YOU COMPOST PET POOP?

 The short answer: yes. But it's not as simple as a typical compost pile or bin you may be using. And you shouldn't use pet-poop compost on your vegetable garden (though it is fine for nonedible, ornamental-only flower gardens.) The reason for this is that compost doesn't reach high enough temperatures to kill pathogens like *E. coli*.

To compost pet waste, set up a separate bin or dig a pit far away from your vegetable garden and use an old garbage can. There are also commercially available animal composters and septic systems.

FIGHT BACK AGAINST FLEAS NATURALLY

  Fleas—yuck. Lots of us may be tempted to grab a noxious can of flea killer to rid the pets and house of these little pests. But there are natural solutions that do not require the use of toxic chemicals. To make an anti-flea spray that is safe for all pets, try this:

---

1 LEMON

2 CUPS (500 ML) WATER

---

1. Slice the lemon into about 6 pieces; place the pieces in a large glass bowl.

2. Boil the water and pour over the lemons.

3. Allow the mixture to sit overnight. After about 12 hours, pour the liquid into a spray bottle. Spray your pet with the mixture, shielding its eyes and making sure to get behind the ears.

"Until one has loved an animal, a part of one's soul remains unawakened."

–Anatole France, writer

GO HERBAL ON THEM

  Before commercial anti-flea products were available, people kept their pets and homes flea-free with herbal remedies. You can avoid the toxic chemicals present in most of these products by making your own natural flea repellent. The herbs lavender, mint, rosemary, sweet woodruff, and cedar are all effective against those pesky jumpers. An easy trick is to tie a bandanna filled with these pungent herbs around your pet's neck. You can make a rub from dry herbs and massage them into your pet's coat. Avoid pennyroyal, which can be toxic, particularly to cats.

CARPET DE-FLEA SOLUTION

 The thought of those fleas jumping around in your rug can induce a murderous feeling. Fortunately, you can eliminate those parasites with an ingredient you almost surely have plenty of—salt! Grab a large handful of salt and sprinkle it evenly over your carpet at night. Just be sure to keep your pets out of the room, because they might lick up the stuff. First thing in the morning, vacuum the salt from the carpet. Approximately every 6 weeks, repeat.

2 WAYS TO CLEAN PET BEDDING

 Your pets can be the source of all kinds of interesting smells. And the one place that these odors all accumulate is on the pet bedding. Harsh chemicals aren't the answer, though. With some all-natural solutions, you can freshen your pet's bedding in no time:

- Sprinkle a 1/2 cup (110 g) baking soda on top of the pet's bedding and let it sit for a few hours. Vacuum the bedding or shake it outside.

- Launder pet bedding and add a 1/2 cup (150 g) of salt to the load. Then, air-dry the bedding in sunshine to further help eliminate odors.

CLEAN UP CLOUDY AQUARIUMS

 If you can just barely see poor Mr. Fizz swimming in your aquarium, it's time to clean the glass. Mineral deposits can cloud aquariums. Avoid using any cleaning products, because fish are very sensitive to pollutants. In addition to being expensive, cleaning products are chock-full of chemicals that can kill those little guys.

Instead, use a handful of non-iodized salt to scrub the glass clean. Make sure it is the non-iodized variety to avoid getting iodine in the tank, which can harm fish. Rinse the tank several times before refilling.

NATURALLY DITCH THE WET DOG ODOR

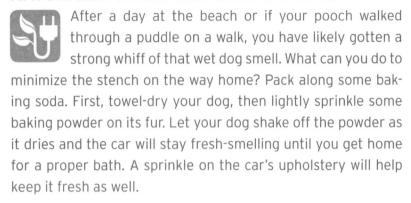 After a day at the beach or if your pooch walked through a puddle on a walk, you have likely gotten a strong whiff of that wet dog smell. What can you do to minimize the stench on the way home? Pack along some baking soda. First, towel-dry your dog, then lightly sprinkle some baking powder on its fur. Let your dog shake off the powder as it dries and the car will stay fresh-smelling until you get home for a proper bath. A sprinkle on the car's upholstery will help keep it fresh as well.

GREEN FACT... In the US and Canada, there are more than 94 million cats and 85 million dogs kept as pets.

Although you may feel that your pet does not use enough energy to make an impact on the environment, when you multiply each pet's energy use by such big numbers, the collective environmental impact is much greater. If every pet-owning household adopted green practices, it would make a big difference for the environment.

THE BEST (AND MOST NATURAL) WAY TO REMOVE SKUNK ODOR

 Did your pooch get a little too friendly with a skunk? Don't reach for the tomato juice. That's a myth. For a surefire and all-natural way to de-stinkify your dog, try this recipe:

---

1 QUART (1 L) HYDROGEN PEROXIDE

1/4 CUP (55 G) BAKING SODA

1 TEASPOON (5 ML) DISH SOAP

Stir the hydrogen peroxide, baking soda, and dish soap in a bucket. Put on latex gloves and wash your dog, working the mixture well into the fur, especially where sprayed. Avoid letting the mixture come into contact the animal's eyes (or your own). Allow the mixture to stay on the dog's fur for about 10 minutes, and then rinse thoroughly with fresh water. While washing, check your dog for any bites or serious scratches (and take it to the vet if you find any). Once finished, don't store the mixture in a sealed container, as it will bubble up and break any containers.

DEICE WITHOUT HARSH CHEMICALS

 During the winter, you want your sidewalks and driveways to be free of ice. But many conventional deicers are made of chemicals such as chlorine salt that can hurt pets (and children) and aren't very good for the environment, either. Some of these chemicals can leach into the ground and contaminate drinking water.

Instead, look for pet-safe deicers. Rather than traditional salt-based formulas, these may be composed of a magnesium chloride hexahydrate-based solution and others may contain time-released fertilizer that helps offset the damage done to vegetation.

GREEN FACT... Dogs produce about 274 pounds (125 kg) of waste a year.

Multiply that figure by the 77.5 million dogs owned in the United States alone, and that's a lot of doggy doo. When Fido goes for a walk, be sure to carry along biodegradable bags. Some bags may claim to be environmentally friendly, but be sure by looking for labels that say they're 100 percent biodegradable and 100 percent compostable.

GROW YOUR OWN CATNIP

 Who knows where that store-bought catnip comes from? It may have also been sitting on shelves for months and months. For many cats, fresh stuff is better. The good news: catnip is easy to grow, indoors or out.

Catnip comes from the plant *Nepeta cataria* (also called catmint, because it's a member of the mint family). In soil that's well drained, start catnip seeds inside during springtime. As the seedlings begin to sprout, keep them away from your kitten. They are delicate and Mr. Fluffy probably doesn't know how to play nice with these baby plants. You can grow catnip inside if you have a window that receives six hours or more of sun per day. Otherwise, transplant the seedlings outside about 12 inches (30 cm) apart.

The soil should be moist and the plants trimmed to allow airflow through the center, because catnip may develop mildew. Once the plant is about 8 inches (20 cm) high, it can be harvested. Just wait until the morning dew has burned off before cutting. Dry the leaves in a dehydrator or oven.

One word of caution for indoor catnip growers: Sometimes it may smell like skunk.

MEMO TO CAT: SCRATCH ON THIS

 Your cats love finding new stuff to scratch. Sometimes it's the back of your old couch. Or it might be the new wallpaper you just paid lots of bucks to hang. Yet, paying for cat scratchers seems silly. After all, aren't the ones in stores just glorified cardboard? You bet.

Here's how to make your own cat scratcher for next to nothing:

1. **FIND SOME CARDBOARD.** Just about any cardboard box will work, but the bigger, the better for this project.

2. **CUT STRIPS.** With the cardboard ridges perpendicular to your cuts, slice several strips of cardboard that are uniform in size-about 2 1/2 to 3 inches (about 6 cm to 8 cm) wide.

3. **TIGHTLY ROLL FIRST STRIP.** Start rolling one of the strips in a tight circle. The cardboard should be doubled-back on itself so tightly that there's no space in the center.

4. **TAPE STRIPS AND REPEAT.** Once the strip is tightly rolled, tape it closed. It should start looking like a disc now. Continue adding strips of cardboard until the circle is about a foot and a half (45 cm) wide. Tape last strip securely.

BUILD HAMSTERS AN ALL-NATURAL ENVIRONMENT

 These small furry fellows need bedding material with which to make their own nests. It may be tempting to use whatever's handy, but there are a few dos and don'ts when it comes to hamster bedding–for both the little guy's environment and ours.

DO USE

ASPEN WOOD SHAVINGS. Unlike other type of tree shavings, aspen wood doesn't give off any potentially harmful fumes.

CAREFRESH. A wood pulp kind of bedding that is absorbent, yet dust- and odor-free. It's also easy to clean up.

DON'T USE

NEWSPAPER. Once the little guy puts his teeth into newspaper, he can end up eating some–along with the ink. And that can be harmful to hamsters.

CEDAR AND PINE. Shavings from these trees have chemicals that may cause respiratory and other health problems.

STUFFING. Sort of like what you'd find inside a stuffed animal, cellulose or fluffy bedding can block the digestive system and cause choking.

AN EGGSCELLENT IDEA—RAISING CHICKENS

 It may be a stretch for some people to think of chickens as pets because they're not as cuddly as puppies or as cute as kittens. But chickens can be productive members of your family. That's right, eggs. Some people swear by fresh eggs. And with four or five egg-laying chickens, you probably would never need to pick up another carton at the store again.

Here's what you need to know about raising chickens:

CHECK LOCAL ORDINANCES. Cities, towns, provinces, and counties may have rules about whether or not you can have chickens. Some may require coops to be in backyards, others may limit the number of chickens. Be sure and check both local and larger government agencies' rules.

PLAN FOR SPACE. At the bare minimum, you'll need about 12 square feet (about 3.7 square meters) for both a house and run. The house should be at least 2 square feet (61 square cm). The rest should be open space. Another way to plan for space: at the very least, 4 square feet (1.2 m) per bird.

BUILD A COOP. For egg-laying chickens, a small A-frame would be good. It should contain a nesting box. The yard area enclosing the chicken should have screening or a wire fence that's at least 6 feet high (1.8 m). And if there's a potential for predators, the top will need to be enclosed, too.

PICK A CHICK. Get in touch with a local farm that sells chickens. The best laying varieties include: Australorps, Leghorns, Orpingtons, and Rhode Island Reds. If you're new to raising chickens, start with juvenile hens. They'll start laying eggs soon and will be less prone to disease.

PROVIDE FEED AND WATER. Be sure to keep water available to the coop at all times for chickens. And most who raise chickens find it easier to keep food available at all times, too. Simply throw more feed (which is usually a combination of wheat and cracked corn) in the coop when the supply looks low.

COLLECT YOUR EGGS. At about 4 to 6 months old, hens begin laying.

"Ever consider what pets must think of us? I mean, here we come back from a grocery store with the most amazing haul —chicken, pork, half a cow. They must think we're the greatest hunters on Earth!"

—Anne Tyler, novelist, author of *The Accidental Tourist*

Green Family 101:
ENSURE PET TOYS ARE SAFE AND ECO-FRIENDLY

Pet toys may seem like an indulgence (to non-pet owners) but they're actually necessary to keep most pets healthy and happy! Not only do toys encourage play, they relieve boredom in pets left at home alone, curb problem behaviors, and help in training. And if you are a pet owner, you know that pets play hard with their toys, chewing, scratching, and often ripping them to bits.

Yet pet toys are often made and purchased without thought. Pet toys are frequently designed to capture the interest of the owner browsing in a store than with the needs of the pet in mind.

Indeed, it may surprise you to discover that you need to be careful when buying toys for Fido and Mr. Whiskers. There are no laws or standards regarding the manufacture of pet toys, and no safety regulations to restrict the use of toxins (such as lead) or unsafe materials. To further complicate matters, many pet toys come from manufacturers in far-flung countries, where it's even harder to determine what kind of material that squeaky squirrel is made of.

Fortunately, a new wave of pet toys has begun to hit the market. As pet lovers have become aware of the dangers posed by unregulated toys, pet-toy makers have started to make toys that are truly animal-friendly thanks to consumer demand.

When you shop for pet toys, look for the same assurances you seek out in children's toys and other products. Because there are no regulations as yet, you will have to rely upon the manufacturer's claims. Look for specific phrases such as:

- **Nontoxic materials, dyes, colors, pigments**
- **Organic materials**
- **Safety-tested**
- **Pthalate-free, lead-free, BPA-free**
- **Free of cadmium, mercury, and hexavalent chromium**
- **All-natural rubber**
- **FDA approved (i.e., safe to eat)**
- **Conforms to ASTM guidelines (like children's toys) or CPSIA (Consumer Product Safety Improvement Act)**
- **GOST (Global Organic Textile Standard)**

Remember, too, that how you clean your pet toys can affect your animal's health—and your household environment. When you need to wash off the dried-on slobber from doggy's favorite rubber ball, skip the conventional, chemical-based cleanser in favor of plain old water. For a really dirty object, mild dish soap can be used, but be sure to rinse thoroughly. Also, avoid detergents with fragrance or dyes when washing their bedding.

ENTERTAIN A CAT FOR HOURS

   Skip the cat toy aisle the next time you're at the pet store. With just a little sewing know-how and some catnip, you can keep your kitten happy and playful.

---

1 CUP (220 G) DRIED CATNIP

1 OLD PAIR OF JEANS

THREAD

---

1. From the old jeans, cut two 3-inch (8 cm) squares.

2. Place one on top of the other, and sew three sides securely closed.

3. It should now look like a little denim pocket. Flip it inside out, then fill with catnip. Add a little bell if you want to be fancy.

4. Sew the open side closed, and your cat is ready for some fun.

"I am in favor of animal rights as well as human rights. That is the way of a whole human being."

—Abraham Lincoln

BRAID A SIMPLE DOG CHEW TOY

  Reduce your dog's carbon footprint by not buying new toys. Instead, you can make things your puppy will enjoy chewing on. Old dish towels are perfect for this craft.

1. First, gather three clean, old dish towels of about the same length.

2. Snip about an inch-wide (2.5 cm) swath of cloth from each towel. Roll the towels and scrunch together, then use one of the small strips to tie one end.

3. Braid the three towels together, cinching along the way to ensure it's very tight.

GREEN FACT... Pets are big business, with owners spending billions (yes, with a B) on furry friends.

About 63 percent of dog owners and 58 percent of cat owners give holiday presents to their animals. Each year, Americans spend about $5 billion on these pet presents. Also, more than one-third of dog owners and one in five cat owners give their pet birthday presents.

CHAPTER SEVEN

Working & Traveling Green

WORKING AND TRAVELING GREEN

Incorporating eco-consciousness into our daily lives can be a challenge—how to be green at work and at play? The key is finding ways to reduce your energy and resource consumption while going about your everyday activities. Your car may be your biggest polluter, and probably represents the biggest challenge to living green, but even if you have to drive, there are lots of ways to lessen the impact. Choosing the smallest, most fuel-efficient model or opting for a hybrid or electric model are two good places to start. Traveling longer distances? Here are ideas on making your trips more sustainable. And when it's time to head back to the office, you'll find there are lots of ways to be greener in your working life, too, and this chapter supplies a wealth of tips.

USE PUBLIC TRANSPORTATION

  Spend less time in the car and save the planet! If walking or biking to your destination isn't an option, consider taking public transportation. Driving less reduces your carbon footprint, saves you money, and promotes a healthier lifestyle.

The average American household spends 16 cents of every dollar on transportation, almost 95 percent of which is spent on buying, maintaining, and operating cars, according to the American Public Transportation Association. They conducted a study showing that households that use public transportation instead of driving can save an average of $9,000 per year.

And how much will your switching from driving to public transportation save in resources? It's complicated, but a couple of facts can give you an idea:

- By eliminating a second car and using public transportation instead, a household's carbon emissions can be reduced by up to 30%.

- In the United States alone, public transportation saves some 4.2 billion gallons (16 billion L) of gasoline (about 45 million barrels of oil) each year. This is roughly the energy needed to power a quarter of all American homes annually.

So if you live in a place that has a decent public transportation system, use it!

Green Family 101:
HOW TO COMMUTE TO WORK BY BIKE

  Ride your bike to work and you turn into a green superhero. Not only are you reducing the amount of carbon dioxide in the atmosphere, but the exercise helps you lose weight and reduces your risk for a whole host of health problems.

In some cities, bike commuting may even be faster than driving. Studies have shown that for trips of less than 3 miles (5 km), it may be quicker to ride a bike than drive a car. Bike commuting is a lot simpler than you might think. Here's how to overcome the most-common obstacles when riding to work.

ROUTE. The way you drive to work may not be ideal for cycling. Use a biking map app to check for bike lanes and plan an alternative route, or ask at the nearest bike shop for someone to help you figure it out. If you have to take the kids to school, you can also drive them if necessary, then cycle from there to work. Or, all of you can ride together!

WORK CLOTHES. If you need a different set of clothes to work in, on the first day of the week, drive to work with your bike in the car, bring several sets of work clothes, and leave them at the office to change into. Bike home, then back to work the next day.

SHOWER. If there's no place to shower at your work, look into joining a nearby gym. For an even easier and quicker way to de-stinkify: baby wipes. Just wipe yourself down in the bathroom upon arrival, and no one will notice anything but your healthy glow.

SECURITY. Check to see if there's an unused room or other place to store your bike during the day. If not, a secure lock with a combination (so you don't lose a key) should keep your bike safe.

SAFETY. Wear a helmet. Get it professionally fitted at a bike shop: It should fit snugly and level on your head with the side straps making a V on either side of your ears. It should be tight enough so that only two fingers can be slid under your chin and the strap. Wear it every single time you ride.

COMFORT. Get bike shorts. Padded and fitted, they'll save some wear and tear on your tushie. And, specially for rides longer than a couple miles, padded gloves will help absorb the shock from the road.

CARGO. As you get serious about bike commuting, you'll want to bring more stuff with you. Some riders prefer the on-bike carrying system of panniers, while others opt for a backpack.

NAVIGATE THE ROAD TO BUYING A GREEN CAR

 More and more automakers are adding models that use new technology to make the most of fuel. Now, some cars get plugged in instead of filled up at the gas station. To sort out the different types of cars and to help find the car that meets your needs and is environmentally friendly, you should be up to date on different kinds of cars. To help, here's your alternative fuel guide:

BIODIESEL: Made from animal fats, vegetable oils, and recycled restaurant grease, this fuel works the same as diesel fuel. However, it produces less pollution and reuses those resources, reducing waste.

COMPRESSED NATURAL GAS: Utilizing the same natural gas that also heats homes, these vehicles produce less greenhouse gases. In addition, fuel is about half the price of conventional gasoline. Cars powered by natural gas are still being developed and may be limited because of few places to refill.

"Travel is fatal to prejudice, bigotry, and narrow-mindedness."

—Mark Twain from *The Innocents Abroad*

ELECTRIC: With motors powered by batteries, these cars produce no emissions and require less maintenance than gas-powered vehicles. With newer models, driving range continues to increase.

HYBRID: Combining electric and gas, hybrids can switch between power systems depending on driving conditions. This kind of fuel use saves money and means that the gas tank may not need filling. Hybrids are good choices for those who have to navigate stop-and-go city traffic.

HYDROGEN FUEL CELL: In these vehicles, an electrical motor is powered from a chemical process using hydrogen and air. The only emission is environmentally friendly water vapor.

"Three Rules of Work: Out of clutter find simplicity; From discord find harmony; In the middle of difficulty lies opportunity."

–Albert Einstein, physicist

KEEP YOUR CAR RUNNING CLEAN

 If you have to use a car regularly, there are several things you can do to ensure that it's running in peak shape and making a smaller impact on the environment. In addition to reducing the amount of carbon dioxide a car emits, these tips will help lengthen the life of a car, which means fewer cars in the scrap heap.

- **PROPERLY INFLATE TIRES.** If your tires aren't inflated to the correct air pressure that's shown on the sidewall, your fuel consumption may be 3 percent higher than it should be.

- **REDUCE SPEED.** The seconds you save going a little faster aren't worth the damage to the environment or the cost. For example, laying off the gas from 70 mph to 50 mph (100 to 80 kph) will use one-quarter less fuel.

- **COORDINATE ERRANDS.** Instead of multiple trips, run all your errands at once, and check with friends to see if they want to go, too.

- **LAY OFF THE PEDALS.** Don't rev the accelerator, then slam on the brakes. A smooth, steady driving style decreases gas use. Whenever you're on the highway, use overdrive or cruise control.

DON'T BE IDLE

  Allowing a car to sit with the engine running is really a crime against nature—and it may be a crime in your municipality, too, as many local governments are passing laws against idling. Leaving the car on to heat up on cold mornings or while you run into a store is simply a waste. When a car idles, it puts out as much pollution as when it's running, but you're not going anywhere! Remember these two tips for reducing your idling time:

30 SECONDS OR MORE? Turn it off. A car doesn't burn more fuel when it restarts. You can potentially save hundreds of dollars a year by reducing the amount you idle, too.

DRIVE TO WARM UP. With the advanced technology in today's engines, they don't need to warm up, even when it's cold outside. Simply, start driving at a slow, steady pace and the car will be warm in no time.

GREEN FACT... Don't stand idly by.

For every 10 minutes your engine idles, 1 pound of carbon dioxide is released into the atmosphere; idling diesel trucks emit more than 40 types of harmful pollutants.

GREEN YOUR WORKPLACE

    Not every workplace can go green the same way. But, hopefully, a few of the following tips can be integrated into yours. Once some environmental awareness builds in the workplace, others will contribute and it'll be easier to go green.

APPOINT AN EFFICIENCY CZAR. This employee can be charged with finding energy savings and act as a point person for suggestions about going green.

SUGGEST SAVINGS BONUSES. Some companies offer bonuses for employees who come up with energy- and money-saving ideas.

ADD RECYCLING BINS. Place paper recycling bins near copiers and faxes. Don't hide them. Put out bins for plastics, too. Keep the bins visible to remind people to recycle. In some offices, it may make sense for each workstation to have its own recycling bins.

REPEATEDLY REUSE FILE FOLDERS. File folders are practically indestructible. Instead of tossing when the label is used, relabel or tape over it and reuse. This principle may apply to other office stationery items, too—ruined copies can become scratch paper, for example.

CREATE A LAST-ONE-OUT RULE. Whoever leaves the office last should be put in charge of turning off lights and all office machinery that does not need to be left on. Power strips can make this job easier.

INSTALL MOTION DETECTORS. These sensors will turn off lights if there's no motion in a room.

OFFER REUSABLE PLATES, UTENSILS, AND MUGS. Instead of accumulating disposable containers and utensils from takeout, encourage workers to bring lunch. Bringing lunch from home is also usually healthier and produces less waste.

SWAP DESK LIGHTS. Instead of fluorescent desk lights, switch to LED ones.

REUSE TRASH CAN LINERS. Talk to your office cleaners about reusing these plastic liners until they are dirty, rather than simply replacing them automatically every night or every week.

IMPROVE THE OFFICE AIR QUALITY. Just as you would at home, avoid polluting the office air with toxic cleaning products, and while you're at it, consider improving the air quality with the addition of plants.

CHANGE YOUR DEFAULT PRINTER TO GREEN

 The humble home office printer can be a serious waste producer, as it eats up paper, ink, electricity, and other resources. Printer cartridges are an environmental triple threat. If just thrown away, the plastic will stay around for years, and the chemicals in the ink can leach into the ground, plus you'll have to keep buying more.

- **CHECK THE FINE PRINT.** When buying a printer, look for one that accepts remanufactured ink or toner cartridges.

- **RECYCLE USED CARTRIDGES.** Many printer manufacturers and office-supply stores will exchange old cartridges.

- **RECHARGE CARTRIDGES.** Some ink manufacturers provide kits that allow you to add new ink to cartridges.

- **GO ALL-IN-ONE.** Instead of having a separate copier, scanner, and fax, shop for an all-in-one machine.

- **LOOK FOR REFURBISHED.** Save money and resources with refurbished equipment.

- **USE FAST PRINTING.** This setting allows lower ink usage.

- **ALWAYS PREVIEW BEFORE PRINTING.** Check out the previews before pressing that print button; print duplex (2-sided) when possible.

YOUR NEW COMMUTE:
WALKING DOWN THE STAIRS

 Just think: During the time you usually spend weaving through morning traffic, you could already be at your desk working. Your desk at home, that is.

With innovations such as video conferencing, instant messages, and cloud computing, telecommuting is easier than ever before. The only trick may be getting your company to agree. Here are a few consideratons:

- When crunched for space or moving to a new space, a company may be more receptive to telecommuting.

- Research has shown that telecommuters actually get more work done and are happier and more focused.

- Offer to work from home instead of a raise. The sneaky bonus: You'll be giving yourself a raise because you won't have to pay for gas.

- Offer to work 10-hour days, for four days a week.

- Stay in constant communication. Respond to work e-mails quickly.

FLY THE CARBON NEUTRAL SKIES

 The amount of environmental damage from carbon emissions by planes is significant. And flying from Europe to the west coast of North America, for example, can cause as much environmental damage as commuting locally in a car for a year.

So, to travel green, fliers are going carbon neutral, which means they pay a fee to offset the carbon emissions of the flight. Depending on length of flight, these fees can range from about $10 to $40. The money goes to organizations that use the funds for environmentally friendly activities, such as planting trees to offset the carbon put into the atmosphere from air travel.

GREEN FACT... Planes are about equal to cars in fuel consumption.

When compared per passenger per mile, airplanes produce about the same about of carbon dioxide output. Another way to think about it: 60 trips across the country by car is about the same as one cross-country plane trip with 60 passengers.

PLAN AN ECO-CONSCIOUS VACATION

 When it's time to plan a trip, keep in mind that you can opt to use fewer resources when you travel as well. Follow these tips to help you travel green.

RESEARCH ONLINE. Use travel web sites to research your destination, plan your trip, and provide travel guides to just the places you are going.

FLY SHORT, STAY LONG. Choose a destination that allows you to make fewer plane trips (i.e., a place to which you can fly direct) and stay there longer rather than packing multiple flights into one trip.

REWARD SUSTAINABLE BUSINESSES. Give your business to airlines, rental companies, hotels, resorts, and restaurants that make an effort to be sustainable. For example, a resort that practices water conservation and sustainable landscaping would be a good choice. Many such businesses belong to programs such as Green Seal or otherwise promote their sustainability.

DON'T DRIVE. Go on a bike or walking tour or use public transportation such as railways, subways, and buses.

ROAD TRIP ESSENTIALS

   Ahhh, the great open road where families bond by playing I Spy and hoping bladders hold until the next rest stop. In addition to a lot of parental patience, here are some suggestions about what to take with you on the road to be environmentally conscious:

PICNIC BASKET. Pack your snacks, along with a set of reusable plates, silverware, and cups. Instead of buying junk food and using disposable utensils at every rest stop, use the ones you brought, and just rinse them off at the rest stop.

REUSABLE BOTTLES. Bring your own water or other drinks in your own reusable bottles. Pack enough that you won't have to refill (a good safety measure, too). If you do drink it all up, refill your water at the rest-stop fountain.

TRASH BAGS. One can be used to collect recyclable products, the other can be used for waste, like that half sandwich that no one wants.

ORGANIC SNACKS. Don't rely on gas station junk food, with its plastic packaging and plastic taste. Portable fruit such as apples and oranges make for healthy on-the-road snacks.

THINGS TO DO BEFORE YOU LEAVE

 When you leave for a trip, you leave your cares behind. But taking a few small steps at home before you leave means you avoid wasting energy and money:

- Unplug appliances and electronics such as televisions and computer monitors.

- Turn off the freezer's ice maker.

- Adjust the thermostat so your heating or cooling system isn't used as much while the house is empty.

- Offer your newspaper to a neighbor while you're gone or stop delivery.

- Set the water heater on lowest setting.

"The secret of joy in work is contained in one word—excellence. To know how to do something well is to enjoy it."

—Pearl Buck, author

RENT CARS WITH A CONSCIENCE

 If you can avoid owning a car, good for you! There may still be times that you need one, however, such as when you take a road trip, and that usually means renting. Luckily, car rental companies have heard customers' calls for more environmentally friendly options. Several major car-rental companies around the world offer a host of options, including:

- Hybrid rentals

- Electric car rentals

- Specific fleets of fuel-efficient vehicles

- Offsets for carbon emissions

In addition to rental car companies themselves, you can find green rental options at travel sites, too.

> "Every time I have some moment on a seashore, or in the mountains, or sometimes in a quiet forest, I think this is why the environment has to be preserved."
>
> **−Bill Bradley, American politician**

HOW TO HAVE A GREEN HOTEL STAY

 No matter where you and your family bed down while traveling, you can make your stay a little more environmentally friendly.

HIT THE OFF BUTTON. If you leave the room, be sure that the lights, television, and especially the air-conditioning and heat are turned off.

FIND RECYCLING BINS. Just because you're on vacation doesn't mean your family's earth-friendly habits should stop. Check the hotel's guidebook or call the front desk to find out how to recycle plastics and paper.

HANG TOWELS NEATLY. Choose a hotel with a linen and towel reuse program, and follow the instructions. (Leaving towels on the floor or even draped on the tub usually means you want them replaced.)

ADJUST THERMOSTAT. If you notch down the thermostat a degree or two in winter or up a couple degrees in summer, you won't feel the difference but will save energy.

PRAISE GREEN PROGRAMS. Be sure to thank the manager for recycling or offering green alternatives.

PACK ALONG A NIGHT-LIGHT. No one likes stubbing a toe in an unfamiliar room, but instead of leaving a light on all night, bring along your own low-energy night-light.

LEAVE THE NATURAL BEAUTY FOR OTHERS TO SEE

 From the delicate landscapes of Yellowstone Park in Wyoming to the Galapagos shore, the wonders of the world will only stay preserved if visitors take nothing but photos and leave nothing but footprints. To tread lightly when sightseeing no matter where you go, follow these tips:

JOIN SMALL GROUPS. Tours with fewer participants may make less of an impact on the environment.

SIGN UP WITH LOCAL GUIDES. Tour guides who live near natural attractions may be more likely to be respectful and help preserve the environment.

STICK TO MARKED TRAILS. Venture off the path and you may unintentionally damage some rare foliage, get lost, or have a run-in with some wildlife.

COMPLETELY EXTINGUISH FIRES. Burying a fire may not do the trick. Such fires may continue to smolder and even flare up.

PACK ALONG TRASH BAGS. Carry out whatever you carry in, then some. If you see trash along the trail, pick it up.

BUY LOCAL. In addition to getting to taste local cuisine, you're also supporting the local economy, which is built around preserving the natural attractions.

BOOK AN ECO-TOUR

 Part vacation, part learning experience, an eco-tour is a trip that will raise your awareness about ecological issues while also showing you some of the most beautiful places in the world.

Such trips are designed with the environment in mind. Transportation and lodging often use as few resources as possible and attempt to be minimally invasive within the environment. Tour guides are often experts in specific areas of study, such as marine biology. On such trips you may also see how local people are building with sustainable material to avoid affecting the surrounding, gorgeous environment. And you may take a lesson or two back home in addition to amazing photos.

GREEN FACT... Workers in the United States commute by car an average of 47 hours per year.

All that rush-hour time adds up to 3.7 billion hours a year, equal to each person just sitting in a car for almost two days. The gas used on commuting also amounts to 23 billion gallons (over 87 billion L).

Green Family 101:
TAKE A VOLOUNTEER VACATION

These days, taking a family vacation doesn't necessarily mean heading to a humongous theme park. Folks are increasingly seeking out vacations that give something back. You can find these opportunities close to home or in more exotic parts of the world. With such monikers as "giveback getaways"or "voluntourism," these are sort-of working vacations, where you volunteer your time and talents to help preserve habitat or help people while visiting a new place.

You could rebuild trails in Canada's scenic woods to help prevent erosion. Or you could track the migration of whales in the Pacific Northwest. You can choose to head to Sri Lanka, for example, to monitor elephant herds or to Greenland to track the effects of global warming. To find the right volunteer vacation for you and your family, first ask yourself these questions:

HOW LONG DO YOU WANT TO BE GONE? Some volunteer vacations can be as short as a weekend or may last several months.

ARE CHILDREN WELCOME? For a family vacation, research tours or trips that specifically include kids. References from other families who've tried it are a great source of information.

WHAT'S YOUR COMFORT LEVEL? Are you okay with camping? Is living on a sea-bound boat tolerable? Find out in detail what the accommodations entail to avoid unpleasant surprises.

WHAT ARE THE PHYSICAL DEMANDS? Some trips require more physical labor and ability than others. Be sure that you and your family members are prepared for and comfortable with the demands of the trip.

DOES THE TOUR COMPANY OFFER REFERENCES? Make sure to sign up with a reputable operator, used to working in sensitive environments; the company should have a track record of successful, sustainable trips.

ARE THERE IN-COUNTRY GUIDES? With guides who hail from the country you're visiting, you're more likely to have an authentic experience and be working with a company that's sensitive to the environment.

WHAT KIND OF FOOD WILL YOU EAT? Understand what is being offered in terms of meal plans and what kinds of foods you will be eating. Often a wonderful part of this experience.

Traveling responsibly and participating in a helping adventure can help your family connect in a more authentic, deeper way with the environment and the cultures it sustains.

CHAPTER EIGHT
Marketplace

MAKING SENSE OF THE GREEN MARKETPLACE

You frequently hear the admonition to "buy green," but you also know about "greenwashing" and are a savvy enough consumer to know that not all products that claim to be green are actually doing something good for the environment. It can make navigating the marketplace daunting. What about investing your money–does it make a difference if you put your retirement funds into eco-friendly investments? With tips on understanding product labeling and learning to be a savvy shopper, this chapter will help you sort out how to spend your money sustainably.

> "I think that, today, more so than ever, corporate responsibility is the best strategic as well as financial path the business can follow."
>
> –Jeffrey Hollender, co-founder of The American Sustainable Business Council

PUT YOUR MONEY WHERE YOUR GREEN IS

   In addition to buying sustainably produced goods, you should also think about investing in companies that have earth-friendly and socially responsible practices. Promoting companies that do good by the environment will make you feel better, but here's the really good news: Investing in companies that focus on sustainability can pay off financially, too.

One recent study tracked 180 companies over an 18-year period and found that those adopting sustainable practices outperformed companies that didn't. And not just by a little bit. The difference was striking. For example, every dollar invested in a sustainable company in 1993 would have grown today to more than $22. For non-sustainably conscious companies, that 1993 dollar would have resulted in only $15.

When looking to invest in sustainable companies, remember that the investment tends to pay off over time, as opposed to bringing you quick gains. If you want to green your investments, consult with a reputable investing firm or money manager and make sure they know that sustainability and eco-consciousness is important to you.

INVEST GREEN

 So you want to put your money into companies that practice good environmental stewardship, protect human rights, and are generally responsible corporate citizens. Where to start? There are several levels of sustainable investing; here is an at-a-glance survey to help you select the right option for your money management. Make sure your investment adviser knows how you feel about where your money is going.

SAY NO TO CERTAIN INDUSTRIES. Known as "negative screening," this is an easy way to make your portfolio greener—simply say no to industries that you believe do not have good records in sustainability questions—examples might be tobacco or oil companies.

ADD SUSTAINABILITY CRITERIA. Ask your investment adviser to rank the top choices for your investments based on their sustainability records, then choose the top scorers.

BE SCRUPULOUS. The most stringent option means choosing to invest only in companies that are fully committed to working toward a sustainable future.

HOW TO BE FASHIONABLY SUSTAINABLE

 It may seem that ethical clothing choices and looking fashionable don't really go together—but there are ways to be stylish and sustainable at the same time.

VINTAGE: There are lots of options for buying previously worn clothing, from high-end designer consignment shops to inexpensive thrift shops—any of these is a great option for reducing your consumption of resources, avoiding sweatshop produced items, and maybe coming upon a vintage find that you love!

ORGANIC: Organic clothing is made from cotton, wool, silk, linen, bamboo, soy, and hemp, among other fibers. Not only do you avoid some potential toxins, but you know that throughout its manufacturing process, your organic clothing was kinder to the planet than conventionally made items.

RECYCLED OR SUSTAINABLE FIBERS: Some polyesters are made from recycled plastics; other fibers, such as lyocel (known as Tencel) are made from wood pulp.

CERTIFIED: Seek out brands with certifying labels that mean the clothing has been made organically and ethically, such as Bluesign, GOTS (Global Organic Textile Standard), Fair Trade, Union-made, and USDA Organic.

5 CREATIVE USES FOR TAKEOUT CONTAINERS

   Part of being a smart, eco-friendly consumer is knowing when you can recycle and reuse parts of your purchases that may otherwise get tossed in the trash. One of the easiest things to find new uses for is takeout containers. Here are five ways to keep this plastic out of landfills:

DESK ORGANIZER. Perhaps you need to corral all your paperclips or maybe store some stationery. These easily stackable containers can help you sort office space.

KIDS' ART SET. Find a home for all those stray crayons, pencils, and pieces of chalk. When the muse strikes your little ones, just pass these plastic containers.

LEFTOVERS STORAGE. Buying plastic storage containers can be pricey. These takeout containers are perfect for, well, food. And if you need to pack extra food for family after a holiday meal, you won't miss the containers, either.

PLANT SEEDLINGS. When you have to start seeds inside before planting outdoors, takeout containers make the perfect starter pots. Lids may even be used to help keep heat and moisture in the soil, as well.

You can also help by asking your favorite take-out food providers to use eco-friendly containers.

WHAT DOES FAIR TRADE MEAN?

 Fair trade is a certification that local communities, often in developing areas of the world, have been provided a higher price for their goods before export. The designation helps ensure that fair wages are being paid to farmers and workers, and that those who benefit from the system are committed to sustainable development. A growing variety of products and foodstuffs have fair trade labels. You may first have noticed this designation on coffee or tea, but you can expect to see it on a wider variety of items. Organizations that certify fair trade include Fairtrade International and Fair Trade USA. Buying fair trade products means you're supporting local communities that have a vested interest in preserving their local environments.

"Goods produced under conditions which do not meet a rudimentary standard of decency should be regarded as contraband and not allowed to pollute the channels of international commerce."

–Franklin Delano Roosevelt, 32nd US President

DECIPHERING FOOD PACKAGING

 Sometimes the wording on the front of packaging is pure sales hype; other times it has specific meanings that can help you make more sustainable decisions. Here are some words you'll likely see and what they really mean:

0 GRAMS TRANS FAT: Zero actually means the food contains less than 0.5 grams of trans fat per serving. Some food processors have replaced trans fats with other unhealthy fats such as coconut oil and palm oil.

100% NATURAL: The good news: There are no artificial flavors, coloring, or preservatives. The bad news: Natural foods can be loaded with fat, calories, and sugar, too.

FAT FREE: Contains less than 0.5 grams of fat per serving; "low fat" means 3 grams or less of fat per serving.

GLUTEN-FREE: Products labeled gluten-free contain no gluten, which is a protein found in wheat grains.

HEART HEALTHY: Such foods contain 3 grams or less of fat per serving and have at least 0.6 grams of soluble fiber in addition to being low in cholesterol, sodium, and saturated fat. However, don't only seek out these foods, because fresh fruit and vegetables are very heart healthy but don't have these labels.

LIGHT: Usually, this designation means the food has one-third less calories than another version.

LOW-CARB: If you see these words on a product, watch out. They are more hype than help, because there's no set meaning for the term. Look at the nutrition labels on these products to be sure you know what you're buying.

LOW-SODIUM: These foods have 140 milligrams of sodium or less per serving.

NO ANTIBIOTICS: Milk, poultry, and red meat may have this designation that means the animals didn't regularly receive antibiotics.

NO HORMONES: Hormones may be given to cattle to increase milk production or gain weight. This label means the livestock was raised without hormones.

ORGANIC: There are different designations of organic. A product labeled organic must contain at least 95 percent organic ingredients. And the wording "100 percent organic" means only Earth-friendly methods were used in the production of the item. Organic foods are made without harmful fertilizers, antibiotics, pesticides, synthetic hormones, genetic engineering, or antibiotics.

SUGAR-FREE: These foods have 0.5 grams of sugar per serving or less.

Green Family 101:
DECODING NUTRITION LABELS

Beyond the big, bold letters on the front of the box is the nutrition label. It's there you'll find out what's in your food—as with so many consumer products, the truth is in the fine print.

SERVING SIZE: Describes how many calories in one serving.

SERVINGS PER CONTAINER: Lots of unhealthy foods promote a surprisingly low number of calories per serving, making you think you can eat more of them—until you really look at the serving size and realize it is much smaller than you would be likely to eat.

CALORIES: Remember, this is the number of calories per serving. A bag of chips may have three servings, so you'll need to multiply the calorie number by three to truly know how many are in one bag.

FAT: The front of the package may boast "no trans fat," but it may contain other types of fat, which can be unhealthy, too.

CHEMICAL INGREDIENTS: Long, multisyllable ingredients likely means the product is loaded with artificial preservatives. If the name of the ingredient can't come out of your mouth, the food shouldn't go in your mouth.

TRANS FAT: Unsaturated fat that contains fatty acids, mostly produced by processing liquid vegetable oil to become solid (some trans fats do occur naturally). Trans fat tastes good, but it increases your "bad" cholesterol (LDL) while lowering your levels of "good" cholesterol (HDL), which is why you should avoid it.

PERCENT DAILY VALUE: These are based on a 2,000-calorie diet. If calculating your calories makes you sweat, just stick to foods that have lower percentages of fat, cholesterol, and sodium and higher percentages of fiber, vitamins, and minerals.

CALCIUM, IRON, AND OTHER NUTRIENTS: The amount of calcium and iron must be listed, and other nutrients are optional.

FIBER: Pay attention to the number of grams. Foods that are good sources of fiber have at least 3 grams of fiber per serving. Most women need at least 25 grams per day to stay healthy, and most men need at least 38 grams. Most people eat less than 15 grams per day.

INGREDIENTS: Ingredients are ordered with those with the most weight in the product listed first. The most important ingredients are the first four.

ALLERGEN WARNING: Near the bottom of the label is a space to let consumers know if there are potential allergens in the food.

BEHIND THE NUMBERS OF
PLASTIC CONTAINERS

 That plastic water bottle has a secret code. Take a careful look at the bottle and somewhere you'll find a small number inside the recycling logo. That number tells you what kind of plastic the bottle is made of. Here's your by-the-numbers guide:

1. **PET or PETE, polyethylene terephthalate** Non-leaching and recycled easily, this type of plastic is often used for water and soda bottles.

2. **HDPE, high-density polyethylene** Found in detergent and shampoo bottles along with milk jugs, this plastic hasn't been found to leach and is easily recycled.

3. **PVC, vinyl or polyvinyl chloride** When this non-recyclable plastic is soft, it can leak toxic phthalates and produce airborne chemicals. It's found in toys, shower curtains, and some spray bottles and cling wraps.

4. **LDPE, Low-density polyethylene** One of the most common uses of this type of plastic is for shopping bags, but it's also used for some drink and food containers. It may not be accepted at curbside recycling, but grocery stores may have receptacles for this plastic.

5. **PP, polypropylene** Used in several kinds of food containers, such as takeout boxes, yogurt cups, and baby bottles. It's easily recyclable and doesn't leach.

6. **PS, polystyrene** May leach styrene, which is potentially carcinogenic to humans. It's found in takeout containers, cutlery, and egg containers. Some locales have banned its use and it may not be able to be recycled in curbside programs, but recycling centers accept it.

7. **Miscellaneous other plastics** This kind of plastic has polycarbonate, which leaches bisphenol A, a chemical that acts like estrogen and can disrupt normal hormone function. This number designation also includes bioplastics, which are made from plant-based materials. While not easily recyclable, such plastics can be broken down in high-heat composting operations.

"The hole in the ozone layer is a kind of skywriting. At first it seemed to spell out our continuing complacency before a witch's brew of deadly perils. But perhaps it really tells of a newfound talent to work together to protect the global environment."

–Carl Sagan, *Billions and Billions*

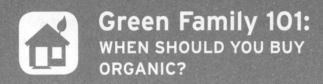

Green Family 101:
WHEN SHOULD YOU BUY ORGANIC?

Maybe you've browsed the organic section of the grocery and noticed that prices of some organic foods may be higher than conventionally produced foods. You know that organic food is grown without harmful pesticides, hormones, or fertilizer. But is it truly worth the money?

Reducing your family's exposure to pesticides is always a good thing. And there are some foods that make a bigger difference to go organic than others. When purchasing onions, for example, you may not reap a dramatic benefit from going organic. But when you choose organic apples, you're ensuring that you're not biting into a fruit with pesticide residue on its skin.

When weighing whether to buy organic or not, there's one simple rule to follow: If you eat the skin of a fruit or vegetable, it's probably a good idea to go organic. At the least, you'll reduce your family's exposure to potential pesticide. One example of why this is a smart buying decision: Non-organic strawberries can retain pesticide residue even after several washings.

12 FOODS TO ALWAYS BUY ORGANIC	12 FOODS WITH LOWER PESTICIDE LOADS
Based on potential pesticide loads, the following foods have the highest loads when conventionally grown and buying organic makes the most sense:	The following dozen foods have a lower pesticide load and can be more safely purchased when conventionally raised:
1. Peaches 2. Apples 3. Sweet Bell Peppers 4. Celery 5. Nectarines 6. Strawberries 7. Cherries 8. Pears 9. Grapes – imported 10. Spinach 11. Lettuce 12. Potatoes	1. Onions 2. Avocado 3. Sweet Corn – frozen 4. Pineapples 5. Mango 6. Asparagus 7. Sweet peas – frozen 8. Kiwi 9. Bananas 10. Cabbage 11. Broccoli 12. Papaya

Resources

GOVERNMENTAL ENVIRONMENT ORGANIZATIONS

A wealth of information about how to save energy and other resources, these government sites also contain country- and region- specific regulations and environmental concerns.

ENVIRONMENT CANADA
ec.gc.ca

EUROPEAN ENVIRONMENT AGENCY
eea.europa.eu

MEXICO SECRETARIAT OF ENVIRONMENT AND NATURAL RESOURCES
semarnat.gob.mx

PARTNERSHIPS IN ENVIRONMENTAL MANAGEMENT FOR THE SEAS OF EAST ASIA
pemsea.org

UNITED STATES ENVIRONMENTAL PROTECTION AGENCY
epa.gov

MAJOR INTERNATIONAL ENVIRONMENTAL ORGANIZATIONS

Pooling information from a variety of worldwide sources, these organizations provide a global perspective on issues such as climate change and pollution.

EARTH SYSTEM GOVERNANCE PROJECT
earthsystemgovernance.org

GLOBAL ENVIRONMENT FACILITY
thegef.org

INTERGOVERNMENTAL PANEL ON CLIMATE CHANGE
ipcc.ch

UNITED NATIONS ENVIRONMENT PROGRAMME
unep.org

BICYCLE COMMUTING

TRANSPORTATION ALTERNATIVES
Transalt.org

LEAGUE OF AMERICAN BICYCLISTS
Bikeleague.org

DEFENDERS OF WILDLIFE
defenders.org

EARTH ISLAND INSTITUTE
earthisland.org

ENVIRONMENTAL WORKING GROUP
ewg.org

FAIRTRADE INTERNATIONAL
fairtrade.net

FAIR TRADE USA
fairtradeusa.org

FOOD ALLIANCE
foodalliance.org

FRIEND A GORILLA
friendagorilla.org

HUMANE FARM ANIMAL CARE
certifiedhumane.org

MARINE STEWARDSHIP COUNCIL
msc.org

NATURAL RESOURCE DEFENSE COUNCIL
nrdc.org

RAINFOREST ALLIANCE
rainforest-alliance.org

RED PANDA NETWORK
redpandanetwork.org

WATERKEEPER ALLIANCE
waterkeeper.org

WHALE AND DOLPHIN CONSERVATION SOCIETY
wdcs.org

BAT HOUSES

BAT CONSERVATION INTERNATIONAL
batcon.org

CARBON FOOTPRINT CALCULATION

CARBON OFFSETS TO ELIMINATE POVERTY
cotap.org

THE NATURE CONSERVANCY
nature.org

"Not all chemicals are bad. Without chemicals such as hydrogen and oxygen, for example, there would be no way to make water, a vital ingredient in beer."

—Dave Barry, newspaper columnist and humorist

CARBON OFFSET VOUCHERS

CARBONFUND
carbonfund.org

POSITIVE IMPACT
positiveimpact.net.au

TERRAPASS
terrapass.com

THE CARBON NEUTRAL COMPANY
carbonneutral.com

CANNING FOOD

NATIONAL CENTER FOR HOME FOOD PRESERVATION
nchfp.uga.edu

COMPOSTING

COMPOST COUNCIL OF CANADA
compost.org

U.S. COMPOSTING COUNCIL
compostingcouncil.org

COMPUTER RECYCLING CENTER AND COMPUTERS & EDUCATION
crc.org

CTIA-THE WIRELESS
recyclewirelessphones.com

EXCESS ACCESS
excessaccess.com

GOODWILL INDUSTRIES
goodwill.org

HABITAT FOR HUMANITY'S CARS FOR HOMES
carsforhomes.org

NATIONAL CRISTINA FOUNDATION
cristina.org

NEW EYES FOR THE NEEDY
neweyesfortheneedy.org

THE SALVATION ARMY
salvationarmy.org

WORLD COMPUTER EXCHANGE
worldcomputerexchange.org

WORLD VISION
worldvision.org

EATING LOCAL

EAT LOCAL CHALLENGE
eatlocalchallenge.com

ENVIRONMENTAL MONITORING

FIREFLY WATCH
legacy.mos.org/fireflywatch/

GREAT SUNFLOWER PROJECT
greatsunflower.org

FARMERS' MARKETS

FARMERS' MARKET COALITION
farmersmarketcoalition.org

LOCAL HARVEST
localharvest.org

"The business of art is to reveal the relation between man and his environment."

–D. H. Lawrence, English novelist and playwright

INVESTMENTS

DOW JONES SUSTAINABILITY INDEX SOCIAL FUNDS
socialfunds.com

SUSTAINABLE INVESTING
sustainableinvesting.net

ORGANIC GARDENING

**INTERNATIONAL FEDERATION OF
ORGANIC AGRICULTURAL MOVEMENTS**
ifoam.org

ORGANIC GARDENING MAGAZINE
organicgardening.com

RODALE INSTITUTE
rodaleinstitute.org

SOLAR ENERGY

AMERICAN SOLAR ENERGY SOCIETY
ases.org

**SOLAR AND SUSTAINABLE
ENERGY SOCIETY OF CANADA**
sesci.ca

VEGETARIAN RESOURCE GROUP
vrg.org

VOLUNTEER VACATIONS AND ECO-TOURS

EARTHWATCH
earthwatch.org

HABITAT FOR HUMANITY
habitat.org

I-TO-I NORTH AMERICA
i-to-i.com

ROAD SCHOLAR SERVICE LEARNING
roadscholar.org

SIERRA CLUB NATIONAL OUTINGS
sierra.org

WILDERNESS VOLUNTEERS
wildernessvolunteers.org

"Like music and art, love of nature is a common language that can transcend political or social boundaries."

–Jimmy Carter, former US president

earth911.com
Several how-to articles on how to recycle, reduce, and reuse along with regular environment-related news stores.

simplesteps.org
Compilation of everyday actions to live a healthier life while preserving our environment.

realclimate.org
Commentary about climate science by scientists, written so laypersons can understand.

recyclenow.com
Advice on how to recycle with a tool that lets you find recycling centers near you.

thedailygreen.com
Loaded with news, recipes, and daily updated.

treehugger.com
With dozens of new posts a day, this site is one of the best sources of green information on the Web.

worldchanging.com
Posts about sustainable living with an emphasis on technology.

ABOUT THE AUTHOR

Doug Donaldson is a freelance writer and editor who regularly contributes articles about health, wellness, and amazingly useful household tips to national magazines. The author of two other books and editor and contributor to several other titles, he was an editor at Rodale's *Bicycling* magazine. An avid backyard gardener, Donaldson lives in the small town of Beacon, New York, with his wife, Liesa; mother-in-law, Beth; cats, Porkchop and Clementine; and dog, Paco.